VOL. 2
CARDIOVASCULAR & RESPIRATORY SYSTEMS

wonders of the
HUMAN BODY

Dr. Tommy Mitchell

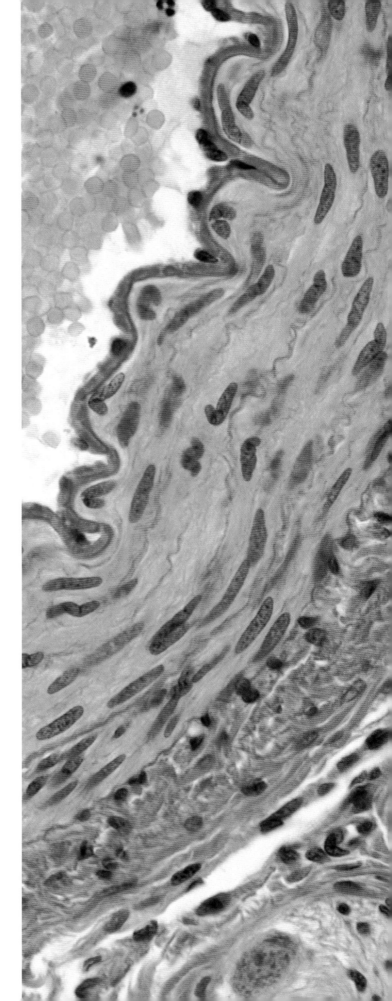

First printing: June 2016
Second printing: November 2019

Master Books,
P.O. Box 726, Green Forest, AR 72638

Master Books® is a division of the
New Leaf Publishing Group, Inc.

ISBN: 978-0-89051-928-8
Library of Congress Number: 2016935317

Cover by Diana Bogardus
Interior by Jennifer Bauer

Unless otherwise noted, Scripture quotations are from the
New King James Version of the Bible.

Please consider requesting that a copy of this volume be
purchased by your local library system.

Printed in China

Please visit our website for other great titles:
www.masterbooks.com

For information regarding author interviews, please
contact the publicity department at (870) 438-5288.

Master
Books®
A Division of New Leaf Publishing Group
www.masterbooks.com

Dedication

*For my three beautiful daughters,
Mary, Ashley, and Sarah*

*Light micrograph of a cross-sectioned muscular artery, showing
a thick and wavy internal elastic lamina, a middle layer with
smooth muscle fibers, and an outer connective tissue adventitia.*

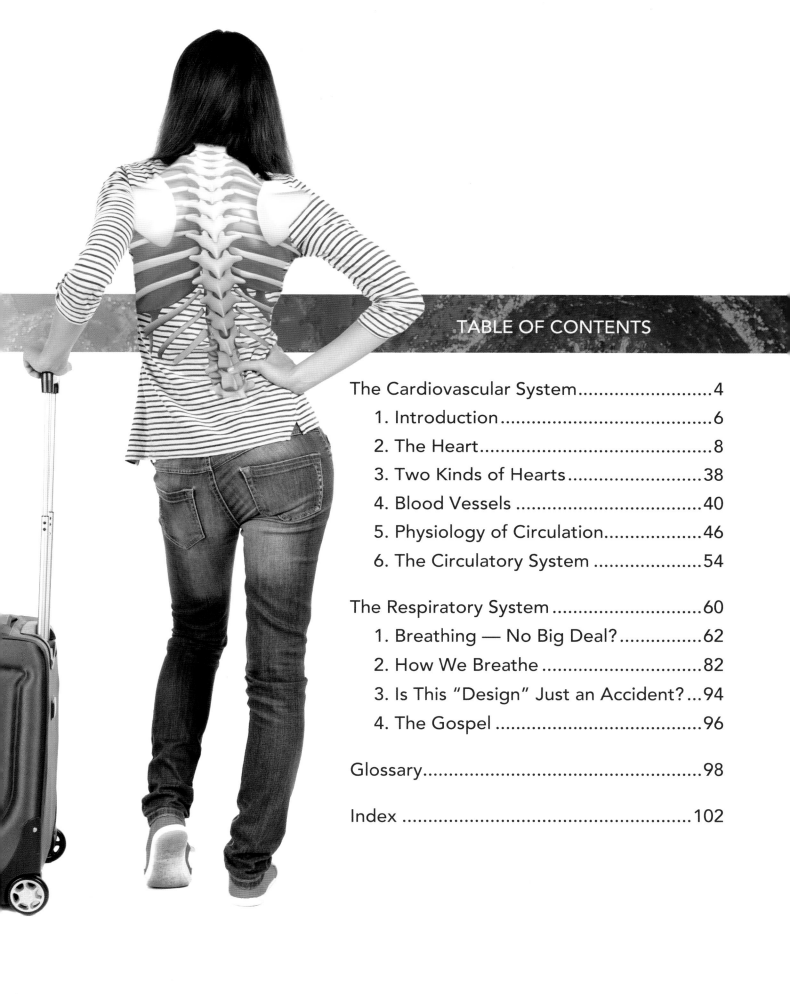

TABLE OF CONTENTS

THE CARDIOVASCULAR SYSTEM

The heart must ceaselessly move blood around your body to keep you alive. It pushes that blood through a system of blood vessels. Those vessels branch out to carry blood all over your body, making oxygen, nutrients, water, and dissolved electrolytes available to every cell in your body. They also carry away waste materials for disposal or recycling. The heart, with all its associated vessels, is called the *cardiovascular system*. This name — cardiovascular — is one of those anatomy word puzzles: cardio- means "heart" and vascular means "vessels."

For You formed my inward parts;
You covered me in my mother's womb.
I will praise You, for I am fearfully and wonderfully made;
Marvelous are Your works,
And that my soul knows very well.
My frame was not hidden from You,
When I was made in secret,
And skillfully wrought in the lowest parts of the earth.
Your eyes saw my substance, being yet unformed.
And in Your book they all were written,
The days fashioned for me,
When as yet there were none of them.
(Psalm 139:13-16)

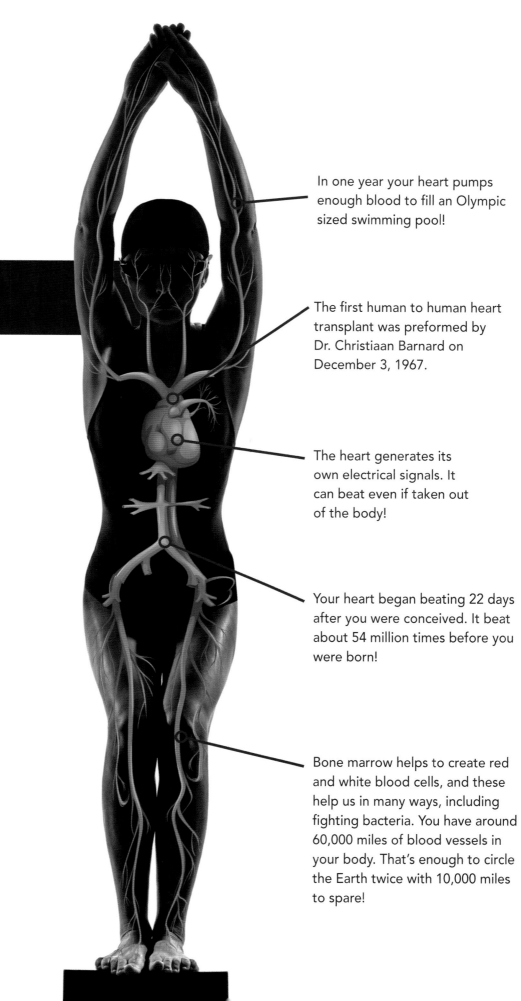

In one year your heart pumps enough blood to fill an Olympic sized swimming pool!

The first human to human heart transplant was preformed by Dr. Christiaan Barnard on December 3, 1967.

The heart generates its own electrical signals. It can beat even if taken out of the body!

Your heart began beating 22 days after you were conceived. It beat about 54 million times before you were born!

Bone marrow helps to create red and white blood cells, and these help us in many ways, including fighting bacteria. You have around 60,000 miles of blood vessels in your body. That's enough to circle the Earth twice with 10,000 miles to spare!

INTRODUCTION

Have you heard your heart beat or felt your pulse? Have you ever blown up a balloon or had your milk "go down the wrong way"? Do you have any idea why people sneeze or cough?

Do you have a friend with asthma? Do you know what a heart attack is? Has someone in your family had heart surgery? Have you wondered how CPR works? Wouldn't it be great to know these things?

The purpose of this book is to explain how God's amazing designs enable your heart and lungs to move blood and oxygen around in your body for a lifetime. Once you understand how these systems work, you'll be able to understand many of the things that go wrong with them and the things you can do to keep yourself as healthy as possible.

  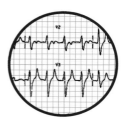 

The human body is a collection of organ systems which all work together to keep you going. Your heart, lungs, kidneys, stomach, and liver are examples of organs. An *organ system* is a group of organs working together to do an important job. Your *circulatory system* consists of all the parts of your body that move blood around. The heart and many blood vessels, large and small, make up your circulatory system.

Another system, the *respiratory system*, gets oxygen from the air; you need oxygen to live. The respiratory system also gets rid of the carbon dioxide your body makes. The respiratory system consists of the lungs and all the tubes (called airways) that air must travel through.

The circulatory (or cardiovascular) system and the respiratory system work together. The oxygen your lungs obtain from the air must be carried to all parts of your body, even into the tiniest places far from your lungs. How these systems work together so precisely is a testimony to our marvelous Creator, the One who designed our bodies with great care.

How We'll Proceed

The body has many organ systems that will be the subjects of other books in this series. But since all parts of the body work together, we'll mention other organ systems a lot. For example, your brain and nervous system help control your respiratory system. We'll talk a little about those systems whenever we need to right here in this book, and then you can learn more about the other systems later in the other books in the Wonders of the Human Body series.

When we learn about an organ system, we first will show you its parts and learn their correct names. Learning the names for things in science is like a puzzle: a lot of the names are built of little words and syllables which help you guess and remember the names of other things in science. We'll use lots of pictures and illustrations to show you anatomy — the way your parts are put together.

Organs are made of tissues, and tissues are made of cells. Sometimes we will show you pictures of what those tissues and cells look like under a microscope, amazing details too small to see with the naked eye. Those "photomicrographs" not only show you the anatomy but also help us to understand how the organs work.

Once you see the anatomy of an organ system and know its parts, you'll be able to understand how the system works. How the systems work is called physiology. When you finish this book, you'll know where the organs are (anatomy), how they work (*physiology*), and what you can do to keep them healthy.

Often, learning about what happens when things don't work right helps us understand how organ systems work in the first place, so we'll discuss some diseases and how they affect the heart and lungs.

In the Beginning . . .

You may have heard that the incredible systems in your body evolved little by little over millions of years, but in fact, God created them perfect and complete in the first man and woman, Adam and Eve, about 6,000 years ago. Their hearts and lungs would have worked perfectly forever if they had not sinned, but disobeying God caused disease and death to enter a perfect world. When we learn about diseases, we are learning about the many things that have gone wrong in the world since Adam and Eve first sinned. In this book we'll talk a lot about the heart that moves your blood around, but in the Bible you can learn about another kind of heart — not the physical heart that beats in your chest, but the invisible heart that can believe in Jesus Christ. Look in the Book of Romans, chapter 10, verse 9. God wants you to pay attention to both kinds of heart.

THE HEART

A normal heart is about the size of a person's fist. It is mostly made of **cardiac muscle**. There are two other kinds of muscle — skeletal muscle and smooth muscle. Muscles that enable you to walk or use your hands are examples of skeletal muscles. So is your diaphragm. Muscles that move your food through your digestive tract and the muscles that surround your arteries in order to allow them to influence your blood pressure are examples of smooth muscles. Cardiac muscle cells are designed to communicate efficiently with each other to pass along the electrical impulses that cause the heart to contract. Cardiac muscle cells are packed with **mitochondria**, tiny power-generators that keep the heart muscle continually supplied with energy. Incredibly, the heart only rests for about a fourth of a second during each "heartbeat." After all, the heart cannot afford to take a break!

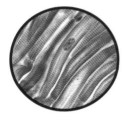   

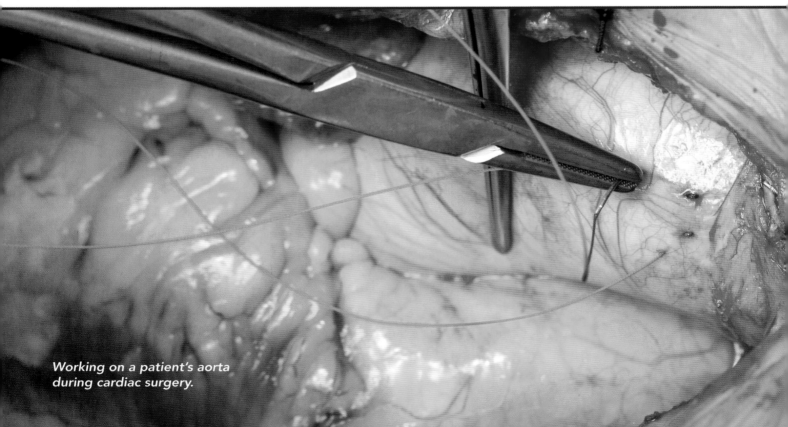

Working on a patient's aorta during cardiac surgery.

The heart in an average adult pumps around 5 liters of blood every minute when resting. In a trained athlete, the heart can pump up to 33 liters per minute during vigorous exercise. On average, the heart moves 7,200 liters of blood per day. You've only got about 5 liters of blood altogether, so you can imagine that the blood circulates throughout the entire cardiovascular system many, many times in a day.

The heart "beats" on average around 72 times a minute when at rest. A young, healthy person's heart may beat up to 200 times a minute while exercising vigorously.

To keep up this steady pace, the many mitochondria in the muscle cells constantly use oxygen to convert glucose (a form of sugar) to energy. Therefore, those cells must be constantly supplied with oxygen. Without oxygen they cannot contract or even survive. If cardiac muscle cells are damaged by lack of oxygen, they have very little capacity to regenerate or replace themselves. Dead cardiac cells are replaced with scar tissue, but scar tissue cannot help pump. When people eat "heart healthy" foods and do "aerobic exercise," they are trying to keep their heart tissues in good shape to work well for a lifetime.

The Heart, a Workhorse

To really understand how much work the heart does, let's do some calculations.

We will base our calculations on a person with an average heart rate of 72 beats per minute. At rest, the heart pumps roughly 70 mL (2.4 ounces) per beat. So . . . if the heart beats 72 times a minute, that means it beats 4,320 times in an hour, 103,700 times in a day, 37,843,000 times in a year. So, in a person who is 70 years old, for instance, the heart has already beat roughly 2,649,000,000 times. That is almost 3 billion heartbeats (yeah, that's billion, not million)!

The average heart pumps 5 liters of blood a minute.

Looking further, if the heart pumps 70 mL per beat, that means it pumps 5 liters a minute, 302 liters per hour, 7,257 liters (1917 gallons) per day, 2,649,000 liters (699,798 gallons) per year. So the heart of our 70-year-old would have pumped 185,431,680 liters (48,985,000 gallons)!

And your heart does all this without taking any time off. It works 24 hours a day, seven days a week. So you would think it wise to keep your heart healthy, right?

Location of the Heart

Your heart is in the center of your chest, under your *sternum*, or breastbone. The heart is shaped sort of like an upside-down pyramid. It is pointed so that its apex is below the middle of your left collarbone. That is why when you put your hand over your heart to say a pledge, you place your hand a little to the left of the sternum, because this is where the "beats" of the heart can be easily felt.

Your thoracic cavity, or chest cavity, has three main compartments. The left and right are occupied by your lungs. Your heart is in the middle one — the *mediastinum*. (The word comes from the Latin word for "middle.") The heart isn't alone in this space. Also in the mediastinum are some important nerves, the large blood vessels (and lymphatic vessels) that enter and leave the heart, and the esophagus and trachea. The esophagus carries the food you swallow to your stomach. The trachea carries the air you breathe to your lungs. There is a lot of traffic in the mediastinum, and with the ever-beating heart the mediastinum is a busy place!

If we look at the mediastinum from front to back at the level of the heart, we'd see the sternum in front, then the heart. Behind the heart is the esophagus, but not the trachea. The trachea splits into the right and left bronchi before it reaches as low as the heart. Behind the esophagus is the descending aorta, and then the spine.

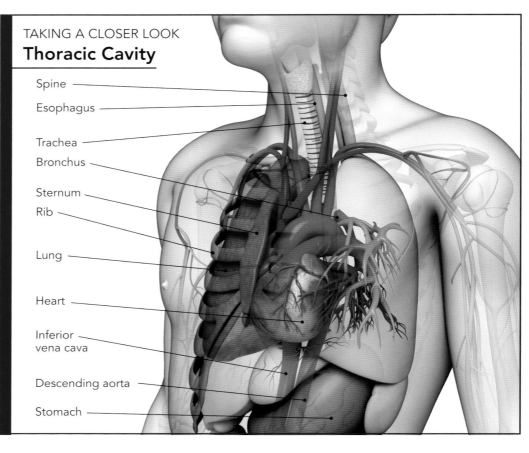

TAKING A CLOSER LOOK
Thoracic Cavity

- Spine
- Esophagus
- Trachea
- Bronchus
- Sternum
- Rib
- Lung
- Heart
- Inferior vena cava
- Descending aorta
- Stomach

Then, below the mediastinum is the diaphragm. The diaphragm is a large sheet of skeletal muscle that separates the chest cavity from the abdominal cavity.

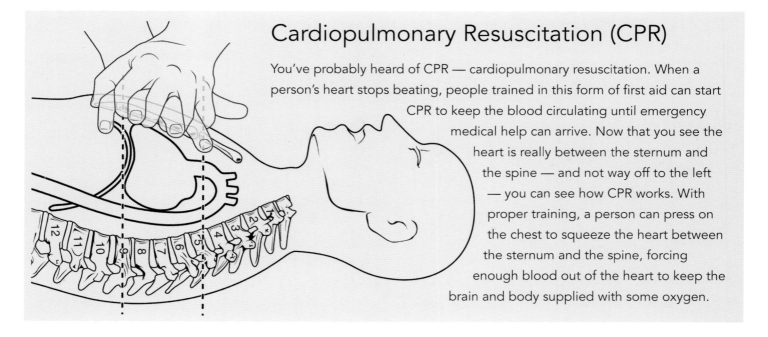

Cardiopulmonary Resuscitation (CPR)

You've probably heard of CPR — cardiopulmonary resuscitation. When a person's heart stops beating, people trained in this form of first aid can start CPR to keep the blood circulating until emergency medical help can arrive. Now that you see the heart is really between the sternum and the spine — and not way off to the left — you can see how CPR works. With proper training, a person can press on the chest to squeeze the heart between the sternum and the spine, forcing enough blood out of the heart to keep the brain and body supplied with some oxygen.

The Pericardium

As the heart pumps, it constantly rubs against the other structures in the mediastinum. You might think that would create a lot of friction. Friction would generate heat and lots of wear and tear on the outer surface of the heart. To prevent this, God designed the heart with its own lubrication system. (After all, blisters from friction like you get on your feet wouldn't do your heart any good!)

Like many other organs that we'll learn about, the heart grows inside a pushed in, double-layered, balloon-like sac during embryonic development. Imagine a slightly inflated balloon containing a tiny bit of lubricating fluid. Now imagine pushing your fist into the balloon so that two layers of rubber are against your fist. Try it yourself with a few drops of cooking oil inside a slightly inflated balloon. Is your hand inside the balloon? Not exactly. But when you wiggle your fist, the oiled rubber surfaces should slide smoothly against each other. The oil prevents friction.

Your heart is inside just such a sac, the *pericardium*. *Peri* means "around." This sac goes around the heart. The *pericardial sac* has an outer layer called the *fibrous pericardium* and an inner layer called the *serous pericardium*.

The fibrous pericardium is composed of tough, inelastic connective tissue. It serves to protect the heart, and to hold the heart in position in the chest.

The serous pericardium itself is made of two layers. The inner layer of the serous pericardium is called

Pericarditis

Occasionally, the pericardium can become inflamed. This condition is known as pericarditis.

It can occur suddenly, and it causes chest pain that is quite often severe. This pain sometimes radiates to the left shoulder and can be mistaken for a heart attack. The inflammation can be the result of a viral, bacterial, or fungal infection. Other causes include malignancy (cancer), heart attack, and trauma.

Normal pericardium
Cardiac muscle
Fibrous pericardial
Pericardial cavity
Visceral pericardial
Parietal pericardial
Pericardial effusion
Pericardium

Some cases of pericarditis are quite mild and are treated with medication that controls inflammation. Other cases can be more aggressive and cause thickening of the pericardial sac, which can limit the movement of the heart. At times, the inflammation is severe enough that fluid begins to collect inside the pericardial sac. (This is called a **pericardial effusion**). Small amounts of fluid are easily tolerated and often resolve with treatment. However, in certain cases the amount of fluid that accumulates in the pericardial sac is enough to compress the heart and alter its ability to pump blood. This dangerous condition is a medical emergency known as **cardiac tamponade**. It is most often treated by inserting a needle into the pericardial sac and draining the fluid.

the visceral pericardium. The *visceral pericardium* is a thin layer stuck to the outer surface of the heart, just like the inner layer of balloon rubber was against your fist. The outer layer of the serous pericardium is called the *parietal pericardium*. The parietal pericardium is fused to the fibrous pericardium.

The visceral pericardium secretes a small amount of fluid, known as *pericardial fluid*, that provides lubrication between the visceral pericardium and the parietal pericardium. This fluid minimizes friction as the heart beats. You see, our Master Designer thought of everything!

If we peeled back the pericardium, we'd see the great vessels emerging from the upper part of the heart. The upper end of the heart is called the *base*, even though it is on the top, because it forms the broader part of the pyramid-like heart's shape. (The *apex* is the pointy bottom end.) Peeling back the pericardium would also reveal the coronary arteries and the cardiac veins running across the surface of the heart and sending their smaller branches down into the muscle of the heart.

The Layers of the Heart

The wall of the heart consists of three layers: the *epicardium*, the *myocardium*, and the *endocardium*. Now you can see how thinking of anatomical names as word puzzles can help you! *Peri*, as in "pericardium," means "around," and the pericardium surrounds the heart. *Epi* means "outer," *myo* means "muscle," and *endo* means "inner." And of course *cardium* means "heart"! Therefore, these words are names for the layers of the heart itself.

Remember, we said that the pericardium consists of the outer parietal pericardium and the inner visceral pericardium, which is plastered to the surface of the heart. The outermost layer of the heart is actually the visceral layer of the pericardium. Where this membrane contacts the heart it is called the *epicardium*. It is made mostly of connective tissue and provides a protective covering for the surface of the heart.

The middle layer forms the bulk of the heart and is called the myocardium. As you might expect, knowing that *myo* means "muscle," this layer

TAKING A CLOSER LOOK
Pericardium and Layers of the Heart

Base

Pericardium

Cardiac veins (blue)
Coronary arteries (red)

Apex

Myocardium

Endocardium

Fibrous pericardium

Serous pericardium

Parietal pericardium

Visceral pericardium

Pericardial cavity filled with paricardial fluid

is primarily cardiac muscle. The myocardium makes up about 95 percent of the mass of the heart. This is the layer that is responsible for the contraction of the heart. There is also some connective tissue in the myocardium. This connective tissue helps hold the cardiac muscle fibers in proper orientation so they can work together to make the heart contract properly.

The innermost layer of the heart wall is a smooth, thin lining called the endocardium. The *endocardium* lines the heart chambers and covers the valves of the heart. It also extends into the blood vessels attached to the heart. Because it is very smooth, the endocardium minimizes friction as blood passes through the heart. Healthy endocardium keeps blood from clotting as it moves through the heart.

Cardiac Muscle

Let's take some time to examine the myocardium in more detail.

In Volume One of *Wonders of the Human Body*, you learned that there are three types of muscle: skeletal muscle, smooth muscle, and cardiac muscle. The myocardium is mainly composed of cardiac muscle. As we will see, cardiac muscle is both similar to and different from skeletal muscle.

Like skeletal muscle, cardiac muscle is striated. However, the striations are not as easily seen in cardiac muscle. Cardiac muscle cells are shorter and fatter than skeletal muscle cells. Also, cardiac muscle cells branch and connect with one another in a somewhat irregular pattern. Like all cells, cardiac muscle cells are surrounded by a plasma membrane

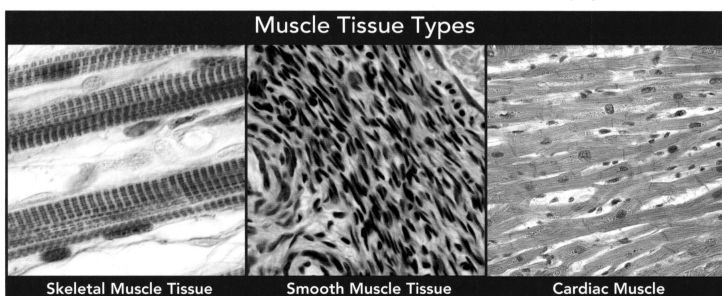

Muscle Tissue Types

Skeletal Muscle Tissue	Smooth Muscle Tissue	Cardiac Muscle
Skeletal muscle is attached to the bones of the skeleton. When it contracts, it allows us to move our arms and legs, or grasp something with our hands, or smile when we're happy. It has a structure that is distinct from other types of muscle.	Smooth muscle is found in the walls of most of the hollow organs of the body. For example, it is found in the walls of our digestive tract where it helps push our food as it is digested. Smooth muscle is found in blood vessels, the urinary tract, the respiratory tract, the prostate, among other places. Smooth muscle is not under our direct control, and is sometimes referred to as involuntary muscle.	The third type of smooth muscle is cardiac muscle. It is found only in the walls of the heart. This type of muscle is also an involuntary muscle.

(also called a cell membrane). At the end of cardiac muscle cells are thick areas of the surrounding plasma membrane called *intercalated discs*. These intercalated discs form a special interlocking connection between the cells. Each intercalated disc contains two special structures that are very impor-tant to the proper function of cardiac muscle. One of these is called a *desmosome*, which helps hold the muscle fibers together as they contract. Also found in the intercalated disc are *gap junctions*. The junctions provide a route for electrical signals to be trans-mitted from muscle cell to muscle cell. These gap junctions ensure efficient transmission of electrical signals, which allows the cardiac muscle to contract in a coordinated fashion.

Cardiac muscle also differs from skeletal muscle in the number of mitochondria it contains. Mitochondria generate energy for the cell, and even though skeletal muscles need energy, they don't need nearly as much as the heart's muscle. Mitochondria make up about 25 percent of the volume of a cardiac muscle cell. In contrast, mitochondria account for only about 2 percent of the volume of a typical skeletal muscle cell. This, of course, makes perfect sense when you think about it, right? A large part of the time a skeletal muscle is at rest so its energy needs would be low. On the other hand, cardiac muscle is constantly active, constantly beating. The much greater number of mitochondria would give the cardiac muscle the energy production necessary to support this high level of activity.

Skeletal muscle responds to the voluntary control of your nervous system. Your conscious command can make skeletal muscle contract. On the other hand, cardiac muscle is involuntary. It does not require conscious command to contract. It is not under your conscious control. This is really the only way the heart could work. None of us would live very long if we had to think about every heartbeat!

Two Pumps in One

We said the heart is a pump, but really, it is two pumps. The heart is two pumps operating side by side, simultaneously. The right side of the heart pumps blood to the lungs. The left side of the heart pumps blood to the brain and the body. One heart, two pumps.

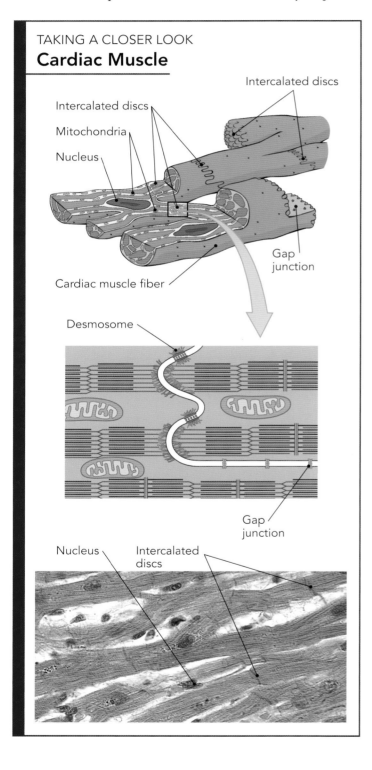

TAKING A CLOSER LOOK
Cardiac Muscle

Intercalated discs

Intercalated discs

Mitochondria

Nucleus

Cardiac muscle fiber

Gap junction

Desmosome

Gap junction

Nucleus

Intercalated discs

The heart's two pumps must be perfectly synchronized. Deoxygenated blood has given up most of its oxygen supply to the body's tissues. This deoxygenated blood returns to the right side of the heart and gets pumped out to the lungs. There it will be resupplied with oxygen. At exactly the same time, oxygenated (oxygen-rich) blood returns to the left side of the heart from the lungs and gets pumped out to the brain and body. If there is even the slightest mismatch between the two sides, problems can develop quickly. A healthy heart is perfectly balanced and keeps blood moving in a coordinated fashion, shuttling it first through the right-side pump, then to the lungs, and then through the left-side pump.

Since the pump on the right circulates blood to the lungs, the right-sided circulation is called the *pulmonary circulation. Pulmonary* means "lung." The pump on the left sends blood to all the body's other *systems*, so the left-sided circulation is called the *systemic circulation*.

We will learn the names for the large blood vessels entering and leaving the heart, but we'll first need to learn the difference between an artery and a vein. An *artery* is the name given to a blood vessel in which blood moves *away* from the heart. When blood leaves the heart to go to the lungs, it travels in arteries. And when blood leaves the heart to go to the body and brain, it also travels in arteries. Of course, the blood going to the lungs is deoxygenated, and the blood going to the body is oxygenated. So the blood in arteries can be carrying lots of oxygen or very little.

Vessels carrying blood *toward* the heart are called *veins*. Now you know that both oxygenated and deoxygenated blood can be carried in arteries. What about veins? The same is true. Some large veins (called *vena cavae* — a word that means big "cavernous" veins) carry deoxygenated blood back to the right side of the heart. And some other large veins (*pulmonary veins*) carry freshly oxygenated blood from the lungs to the left side of the heart. So, as with the

arteries, veins can be carrying blood rich in oxygen or blood with very little.

Confusing, right? Well, we will try and give you a hand.

You may have seen drawings of the circulatory system and noticed that some of the blood vessels are colored red and some blue. Artists often draw the blood vessels this way to show you which vessels carry oxygenated blood and which vessels carry deoxygenated blood. Oxygenated blood has recently passed through the lungs to pick up a full load of oxygen using the hemoglobin in its red blood cells. Deoxygenated blood has already dropped off most of its oxygen supply in the tissues and is ready to be sent back to the lungs to pick up some more. All blood is red, but oxygenated blood is a brighter red and deoxygenated blood has a more purplish-red color. Even though deoxygenated blood is not really

TAKING A CLOSER LOOK
Pulmonary vs Systemic Circulation

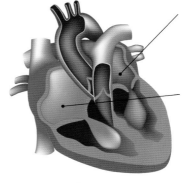

Systemic circulation - The left side pump fills with oxygen-filled blood from the lungs.

Pulmonary circulation - The right side pump fills with oxygen-depleted blood from the body.

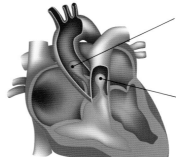

Systemic circulation - The left side pump pushes the oxygen-filled blood to the body.

Pulmonary circulation - The right side pump pushes the oxygen-depleted blood to the lungs.

blue, the blood vessels carrying it are most often illustrated as blue to help people see the difference more clearly.

Chambers of the Heart

The human heart has four chambers.

Two chambers belong to the pump on the right — the right atrium and the right ventricle. These chambers are responsible for circulating blood to the lungs. Again, this is known as the pulmonary circulation.

The other two chambers belong to the pump on the left — the left atrium and the left ventricle. These chambers work to push blood out to the body tissues to supply them with oxygen and nutrients. This is the systemic circulation.

The word *atrium* means "entry room" or "receiving room." The *atria* (plural of atrium) collect blood as it returns to the heart. Blood that has already dropped off most of its oxygen supply enters the right atrium. (This is *deoxygenated* blood.) The left atrium collects oxygen-rich blood returning from the lungs.

Do arteries or veins bring this blood to the heart's atria? Hopefully, you said, "veins." Remember, *veins* bring blood *to* the heart. The veins that bring blood from the lungs to the left atrium are called *pulmonary* veins because they *come from the lungs*. The veins that bring blood back from the brain and the body are called *vena cavae*. The big vein from the upper body and brain is called the *superior vena cava*, and the big vein from the lower body is called the *inferior vena cava*. The name *vena cava* means "hollow vein," and *cavae* is the plural of *cava*. The words *superior* and *inferior* mean "upper" and "lower," respectively.

What kind of blood would you find in the superior and inferior vena cavae?[1] How about the pulmonary veins?[2] See, it's not really all that hard, is it?

The right and left atria collect blood and then send it on to the ventricles. As the atria fill, the pressure within the atria rises as a result of the increasing amount of blood. Then, when the ventricles relax, this pressure starts pushing blood from the atria

---

1 Deoxygenated blood returns to the heart via the superior and inferior vena cavae.
2 Oxygenated blood returns to the heart from the lungs through the right and left pulmonary veins.

TAKING A CLOSER LOOK
Chambers of the Heart

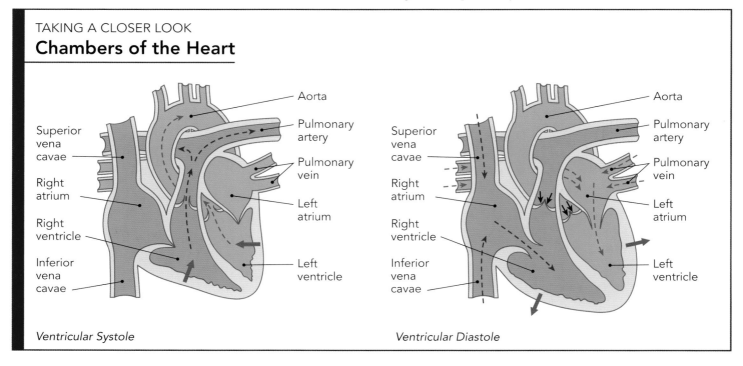

Ventricular Systole   *Ventricular Diastole*

into the ventricles through the valves connecting them even before the atria contract. Just before the ventricles pump, the atria squeeze to push an extra bit of blood into the ventricles. After the atria empty, it's time for the ventricles to squeeze hard and push blood out to the lungs and body.

The right ventricle is part of the pump on the right, and it pushes oxygen-poor (deoxygenated) blood out through the pulmonary artery to the lungs. The left ventricle is part of the pump on the left, and it pushes blood out through a large artery called the *aorta*. This oxygen-rich (oxygenated) blood is sent through the aorta's branches to the brain and to the entire body.

The walls of the ventricles are made of thicker muscle than the atrial walls, but the ventricles are not the same. Remember, the right and left sides must always have the volume of blood they pump in and out perfectly matched. Even though this balance must be maintained, the two ventricles are different from one another. You see, the right ventricle only has to pump blood to the lungs, a short distance away. And it doesn't take much pressure to push blood through the pulmonary circulation. In contrast, the left ventricle pumps blood out to the entire body. It must push blood through the miles and miles of blood vessels that make up the systemic circulation. The pressure in the systemic circulation is much higher than in the pulmonary circulation. Therefore, the muscle of the left ventricle is much thicker than that of the right ventricle. In fact, the muscular wall of the left ventricle is typically two to three times thicker. This thick muscle allows the left ventricle to generate the great force needed to force blood through the entire body.

Pattern of Blood Flow

Now that you've learned about the four chambers of the heart and the major vessels entering and leaving the heart, you should be able to trace the path of blood as it travels through this marvelous

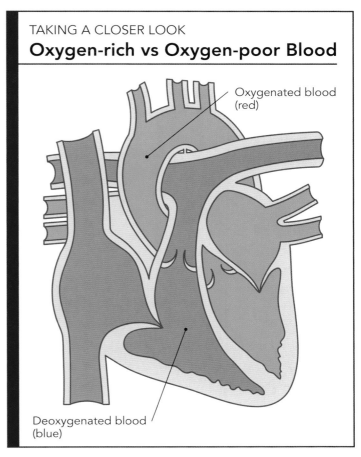

TAKING A CLOSER LOOK
Oxygen-rich vs Oxygen-poor Blood

Oxygenated blood (red)

Deoxygenated blood (blue)

double-pump. Oxygen-poor blood enters the right atrium from the superior and inferior vena cavae. At the same time, oxygen-rich blood is brought by the pulmonary veins to the left atrium. (There are four pulmonary veins, two from the left lung and two from the right lung.) Blood flows from the right atrium into the right ventricle. At the same time, blood flows from the left atrium into the left ventricle.

After each atrium contracts, pushing that last little bit of blood into the ventricles, the ventricles give a mighty squeeze. Oxygen-poor blood from the right ventricle goes out through the pulmonary artery. The pulmonary artery soon branches to the right and left, and each of these subdivides and branches many times to carry blood to the lungs. At the same time, the left ventricle pushes oxygen-rich blood out of the heart through the aorta. The aorta goes upward, sends off some branches, and then arches downward where it continues as the descending aorta to carry blood to the lower body.

Be sure you understand that the right and left pumps fill and then contract simultaneously. Then see if you can trace the path of a red blood cell as it enters the heart, travels to the lungs, returns to the heart, and is sent out through the aorta. Then see if you can do it without looking at the illustrations. If you don't get it right away, relax. It will be easy for you in no time.

Heart Valves

You know that most of the rooms in your home have doors. It is obvious why those doors are there. But are there rooms that don't have doors? Those rooms were designed for a reason. The rooms that have no doors allow access in and out much more easily, right? On the other hand, you've probably seen businesses that have one-way doors — separate doors for going in and for going out.

Which design do you think would work best for the heart's "rooms," its chambers? What would happen to the blood in the ventricles when the ventricles squeezed if the heart's rooms had no doors? If you said some blood would go backward into the atria, you see the problem. The ventricles would waste much of their effort if part of the blood went back-

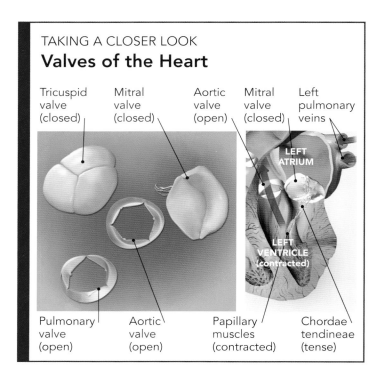

TAKING A CLOSER LOOK
Valves of the Heart

Tricuspid valve (closed) · Mitral valve (closed) · Aortic valve (open) · Mitral valve (closed) · Left pulmonary veins

LEFT ATRIUM · LEFT VENTRICLE (contracted)

Pulmonary valve (open) · Aortic valve (open) · Papillary muscles (contracted) · Chordae tendineae (tense)

ward. To keep this from happening, the chambers are separated by one-way valves. A valve must allow the blood to flow freely in one direction but then shut to stop any back-flow.

Blood passes from the right atrium into the right ventricle through the *tricuspid valve*. Blood passes from the left atrium into the left ventricle though the *bicuspid valve*, also known as the *mitral valve*. Notice that both of these valves have "cusp" in the

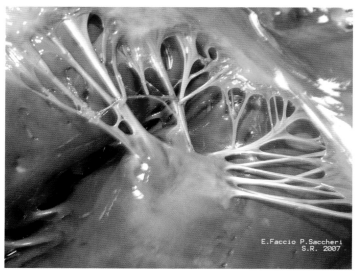

E.Faccio P.Saccheri
S.R. 2007

Chordae tendineae

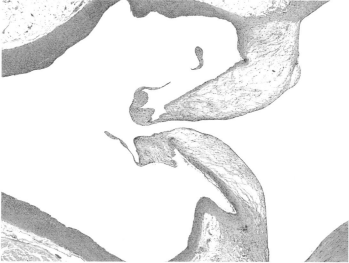

Aortic valve

name. A *cusp* is like a little parachute that fills with blood from the ventricle under pressure, distending the cusp back toward the atrium as the ventricle squeezes. The cusps keep the blood from flowing back into the atria. The tricuspid valve consists of three ("tri") cusps, and the bicuspid (mitral) valve has two ("bi") cusps. The name *mitral* is used for the bicuspid valve because the two cusps look a little like a bishop's headdress, called a miter.

If these cusps were not secured to the walls of the ventricles, the high-pressure blood filling them would push back into the atria. The cusps are therefore tethered to the ventricular walls. The ties that bind these cusps to the ventricular wall are called *chordae tendineae*. This Latin name means "heart strings." As the high-pressure blood distends the cusps, it is kept from being pushed back into the atria by these little tethers.

Already you can probably see the great design in this arrangement. But there could be a problem: when the ventricles contract, they shrink. And as they shrink, the chordae tendineae (heart strings) tethering the cusps must somehow get shorter. Otherwise, the cusps would push back into the atria! God designed an amazing feature to keep the chordae tendineae tight as the ventricles shrink. These little cords are attached to the ventricular walls by tiny papillary muscles. As the ventricles contract, the papillary muscles also contract, being perfectly coordinated with the ventricles. These muscles keep the chordae tendinae taut and stabilize the cusps of the valves. (No way this is just a cosmic accident, right?)

The heart's valves do not require a doorman to close them. The pressure of the blood inside the ventricles pushes them shut. We could even say the pressure makes them slam shut. But they make no noise. You've probably heard that the heart makes a "lub-dub" sound with each beat. The "lub" sound comes from the closure of the tricuspid and mitral valves, but it isn't the "slamming shut" that makes the "lub." It isn't even the silent squeezing of the ventricles that makes the "lub" sound. The "lub" comes from the turbulence of the blood rushing against the valves. (Think of the sound a wave makes as it crashes into a beach. Moving liquids, whether water

---

TAKING A CLOSER LOOK
Heart Sounds

Pulmonary valve (open)

Tricuspic valve (closed)

Aortic valve (open)

Mitral valve (closed)

Ventricle contraction

The first heart sound (S1), is caused by the closure of the mitral and tricuspid valves at the beginning of ventricular contraction (systole)

Pulmonary valve (closed)

Tricuspic valve (open)

Mitral valve (open)

Ventricle relaxation

Aortic valve (closed)

The second heart sound (S2), is caused by the closure of the aortic and pulmonary valves at the end of ventricular systole

or blood, are powerful!) Of course, since the "lub" happens when the tricuspid and mitral valves close, it may be easier for you to think of the "lub" as the result of the doors slamming shut.

When the blood leaves the heart through the pulmonary artery and the aorta, another set of valves is needed to keep it from flowing backward into the ventricles. If any blood flowed backward, the ventricles would have to do extra work by pushing it out again with the next beat. Such an arrangement would not be very efficient! (In fact, this very problem happens when valves are damaged, as we will discuss later.)

These valves — the valves guarding the exit from the ventricles — are called *semilunar valves*. As you know already, *lunar* means "moon," so *semilunar* means "half-moon-shaped." Each "ventricular exit" valve consists of three of these crescent-shaped cusps. The semilunar valve between the right ventricle and the pulmonary artery is called the *pulmonary valve*. The semilunar valve between the left ventricle and the aorta is called the *aortic valve*.

The semilunar valves do not have any chordae tendineae. The pressure in the pulmonary artery and the aorta is not high enough to force them backward into the ventricles, so none are needed.

Just as the tricuspid and mitral valves needed no doorkeeper, the pulmonary and aortic valves need no doorkeeper to open or shut them. Fluid pressure does the job. When the ventricles begin to contract, the pressure they generate slams the tricuspid and mitral valves shut. The pressure in the ventricles then quickly rises, forcing the pulmonary and aortic valves to silently open. The blood in the ventricles rushes out through the open valves. When the ventricles have finished their contraction, the semilunar cusps swing closed and balloon slightly toward the ventricles, filling with blood but not leaking backward into the ventricles.

Heart Murmurs

A doctor often listens to the heart from several locations because the heart sounds transmitted to the chest wall can give a clue about the condition of the different valves. Damaged valves can cause different types of **murmurs**. The location, timing, and type of sound help the doctor know what sort of damage is causing it.

If a valve is damaged and allows blood under high pressure to leak backward, a whooshing murmur may be heard. We say such a valve is **incompetent** because it isn't doing the job a valve is designed for — preventing the back-flow of blood. For instance, were the mitral valve to become incompetent, when the left ventricle contracts, some blood would be pushed back through the valve into the left atrium. The turbulence of the blood passing through the damaged valve would produce a murmur.

If a damaged valve is stiff and does not open normally, the outflow of blood is impeded. This is known as **stenosis**. A whooshing murmur will be heard due to the blood struggling to get through. As an example, if the aortic valve were damaged and became stiff or scarred, it might not open as it should. Then when the ventricle contracts, the blood would not as easily pass into the aorta. Again, the turbulence produced by the forcing of blood through the abnormally small opening would result in a murmur.

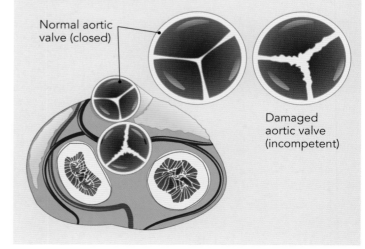

Normal aortic valve (closed)

Damaged aortic valve (incompetent)

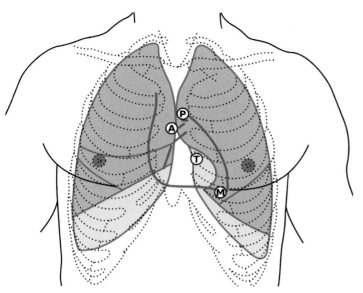

Optimal stethoscope position for listening to heart valves. Heart valves are labeled (Mitral, Tricuspid, Aortic, Pulmonary).

René-Théophile-Hyacinthe Laennec (1781-1826) invented the stethoscope in 1816. The first stethoscope was a simple hollow wooden cylinder. It allowed doctors to listen to the heart and lungs without having to place their ears directly on the patient. Even though that device is primitive by today's standards, it was revolutionary in its day.

If the first heart sound, the "lub," results from turbulence during the simultaneous closure of the tricuspid and mitral valves, what do you think causes the second sound, the "dub"? The turbulence of blood created when the semilunar valves close creates this second heart sound. If you have the opportunity to borrow a stethoscope, you can listen to your own heart's sound. The heart sounds can both be heard at many locations on the chest wall.

The Cardiac Cycle — What Happens In a Heartbeat

The *cardiac cycle* is the name given to the five steps involved in filling the heart's chambers and pumping the blood. We will now examine this process more closely. All five steps must take place — in just the right order — every time your heart beats.

There are specific terms used to describe what a heart chamber is doing during the different steps in the cardiac cycle. The period of time when a heart chamber is contracting is called *systole* (pronounced "sis-tuh-lee"). The phase during which the chamber is relaxing is called *diastole* (pronounced "dī-as-tuh-lee"). Now let's apply those terms — *systole* and *diastole* — to each of the four steps in the cardiac cycle. (Later we will see that these words help us understand a measurement called "blood pressure." You may have even had yours measured!)

The first step in the cardiac cycle is the "filling phase." While they fill with blood, the atria and ventricles are all in diastole. That is, all the chambers are relaxed. Since the heart muscle is relaxed, the pressure inside them is low. This low pressure allows the atria and then the ventricles to fill with blood. First, blood enters the atria. As they fill, blood pushes the tricuspid and mitral valves open, allowing blood to flow into the ventricles too. At the end of this phase, the ventricles are about 75 percent full.

During this phase what do you think is happening with the heart's "exit-doors" — pulmonary and aortic valves? Since the pressure in the ventricles is low at this point, both of these valves will be closed, right? Otherwise, the blood would flow backward into the ventricles. The pressures in the pulmonary artery and the aorta are keeping the pulmonary and aortic valves closed for now.

TAKING A CLOSER LOOK
The Cardiac Cycle

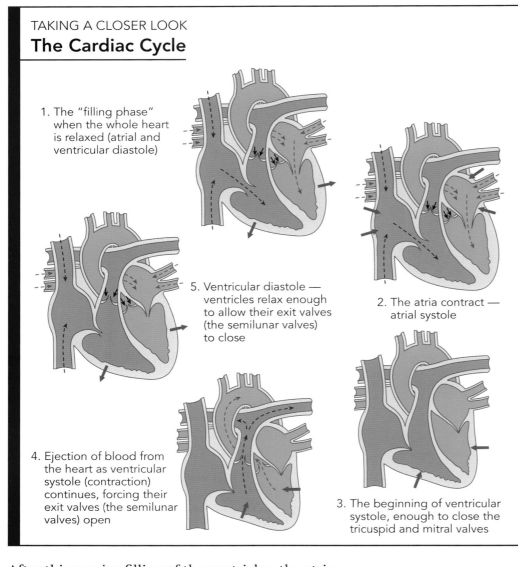

1. The "filling phase" when the whole heart is relaxed (atrial and ventricular diastole)

5. Ventricular diastole — ventricles relax enough to allow their exit valves (the semilunar valves) to close

2. The atria contract — atrial systole

4. Ejection of blood from the heart as ventricular systole (contraction) continues, forcing their exit valves (the semilunar valves) open

3. The beginning of ventricular systole, enough to close the tricuspid and mitral valves

During the fourth step of the cardiac cycle, blood is forcefully ejected from the heart. The increasing pressure from the ventricular contraction forces the pulmonic and aortic valves (the semilunar valves) to open, and the blood rushes out into the pulmonary artery and the aorta.

Finally, in the fifth and final step of the cardiac cycle, the ventricles relax. Because of this relaxation, the pressure in the ventricles decreases. The higher pressure in the pulmonary artery and the aorta causes the semilunar valves to close. Thus, blood is prevented from flowing backward into the ventricles. This is *ventricular diastole*, and it is the end point of one complete cardiac cycle.

So, the five steps in the cardiac cycle are:

After this passive filling of the ventricles, the atria simultaneously contract. This is *atrial systole*. The squeezing of the atria pushes more blood into the ventricles to help really fill them up. This atrial "squeeze" is the second step in the cardiac cycle, and it adds another 25 percent or so to the filling of the ventricles.

Next comes relaxation of the atria (*atrial diastole* — the second step) and then contraction of the ventricles, or *ventricular systole*. During this, the third step of the cardiac cycle, the ventricles begin to contract. As a result of this contraction the pressure in the ventricles increases enough to slam the tricuspid and mitral valves shut, causing the "lub" sound.

1. the "filling phase" when the whole heart is relaxed (atrial and ventricular diastole)

2. the atria contract — atrial systole

3. the beginning of ventricular systole, enough to close the tricuspid and mitral valves

4. ejection of blood from the heart as ventricular systole (contraction) continues, forcing their exit valves (the semilunar valves) open

5. ventricular diastole — ventricles relax enough to allow their exit valves (the semilunar valves) to close

Congestive Heart Failure

The pumping action of the heart is nothing short of amazing. The right side of the heart sends blood to the lungs, and the left side of the heart pumps blood out to the body. Each side pumps the same amount of blood, at the same time, and the process takes place in a coordinated fashion. This precise balance continues day in and day out.

However, we live in a fallen, cursed world. Things go wrong. At times the heart does not function correctly. A heart weakened by disease or heart attack will not be as efficient or pump as powerfully. This is called "heart failure." With heart failure, the heart still works, but one or both of its pumps is weak.

Since the heart consists of two pumps, it is possible for either pump system to function abnormally. If either of the pumps fails to keep up with the amount of blood it is supposed to pump, blood will back up, like cars in a traffic jam. We sometimes say that traffic is "congested," and the same word can be used for blood that backs up due to heart failure. **Congestive heart failure** can be a problem caused by failure of either the right or the left side of the heart to keep up.

If the pump on the right side of the heart fails to pump properly, the blood returning to the heart from the body is not pumped to the lungs efficiently. Then, the vena cavae and other systemic veins that bring blood to them become **congested** with excessive blood. Remember, this is like a traffic jam — traffic congestion — with

blood instead of cars. Blood is backed up. Due to this **congestion**, the pressure in these vessels increases. The most noticeable result of this is swelling in the legs and feet. This swelling is called **peripheral edema**. (**Edema** is swelling caused by fluid accumulating in tissues. **Peripheral** means the swelling happens in parts of the body far away from the heart.)

If the pump on the left side of the heart fails to do its job properly, the oxygenated blood returning from the lungs is not adequately pushed out to the body. Now, if the normal amount of blood is being pumped to the lungs by a correctly functioning right heart pump, but the left heart pump cannot keep up with this volume of blood, what do think will happen? The blood will back up into the lungs! This time the "traffic congestion" backs up into the lungs. This problem is called **pulmonary edema** (fluid in the lungs). Pulmonary edema causes patients to be quite short of breath and make it difficult to exercise or even to walk. In its most severe forms, pulmonary edema can lead to death.

The degree of heart failure can be assessed by the severity of the patient's symptoms, such as shortness of breath or how much exercise they can do. Also, it can be quite helpful to obtain a measurement of the patient's ejection fraction — the fraction of the blood ejected during systole. The lower the ejection fraction, the more severe the heart failure is said to be.

 Treating heart failure is challenging. Patients are often given drugs that cause the body to get rid of the excess fluid that accumulates in the lungs or other tissues. There are also certain drugs that can help damaged cardiac muscle contract more efficiently and make the heart pump better. However, these drugs can also have serious side effects at higher doses, so they must be used cautiously. In certain very severe cases, a heart transplant may even be considered.

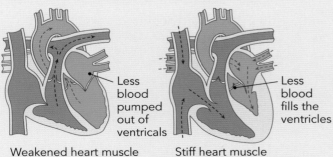

Less blood pumped out of ventricals

Less blood fills the ventricles

Weakened heart muscle can't squeeze as well

Stiff heart muscle can't relax normally

That is what happens every time your heart beats! What do you think happens next? Remember this is a *cycle*, so when the fifth step is completed, the whole cycle begins again. The heart's chambers are all relaxed and the valves are in the right position so that they can fill with blood and the heart can beat again.

How Empty Is Empty?

When you wring out a washcloth or sponge, is it completely dry? No. It still contains some water. You cannot squeeze it enough to make it dry. Likewise, after your heart's ventricles contract, they still contain some blood. Not every drop of blood gets emptied from the ventricles as they squeeze. In fact, a healthy heart only empties around 60–70 percent of its contents with each beat! This percentage is called the *ejection fraction*. If a person's heart is not working properly, its ejection fraction may be far lower than this. Measuring the ejection fraction can be very important for physicians when they are caring for patients with heart problems.

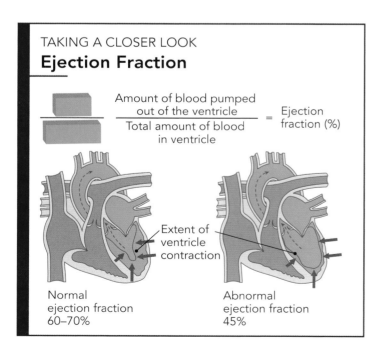

TAKING A CLOSER LOOK
Ejection Fraction

$$\frac{\text{Amount of blood pumped out of the ventricle}}{\text{Total amount of blood in ventricle}} = \text{Ejection fraction (\%)}$$

Extent of ventricle contraction

Normal ejection fraction 60–70%

Abnormal ejection fraction 45%

What the Heart Needs

The heart pumps oxygen-rich blood to every organ in the body. But how does the heart get the oxygen-rich blood it needs? After all, the heart needs a constant supply of oxygen and fuel (in the form of sugar called glucose) in order to keep pumping constantly, day in and day out, for a lifetime! Therefore, God designed the *coronary circulation* — a way for the heart to pump blood to itself.

When something goes terribly wrong with the coronary circulation, a person can have a heart attack. You may know of someone this has happened to. Once you see how the coronary circulation works and why it is so important, you will understand what a heart attack is.

You might wonder why the heart needs its own separate blood supply. After all, the heart is a pump that pumps blood. It is filled with blood most of the time. So why can't it just get the things it needs from the blood in its chambers?

What it comes down to is this: because the heart works constantly, it needs *lots* of oxygen and nutrients. Even though the left ventricle is filled with oxygen-rich blood, the heart wall is just too thick for nutrients to seep into it. A more efficient system is needed to supply the heart muscle — the *myocardium* — with oxygen and fuel.

The *coronary circulation* is a system of arteries and veins that delivers oxygen-rich blood to the heart muscle and carries away deoxygenated blood.

The coronary circulation begins just past the aortic valve. Right after the place where blood exits the heart's left ventricle, two arteries branch from the very first part of the aorta (called the *ascending aorta*). These are the *right and left coronary arteries*. They divert a little of the blood flowing into the aorta toward the heart's muscular walls.

TAKING A CLOSER LOOK
Coronary Circulation

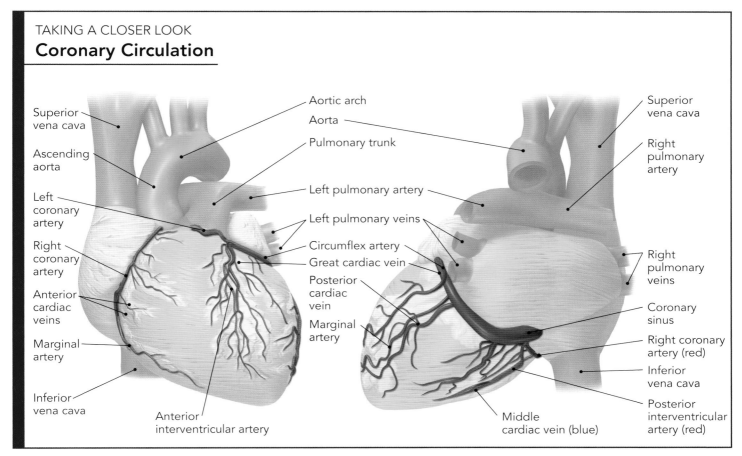

The *right coronary artery* primarily supplies the right atrium and the right ventricle. It divides and divides into many smaller arterial branches to completely supply the right side of the heart.

The *left coronary artery* supplies the left side of the heart. It has two major branches. One of these — the left anterior descending artery, or LAD — supplies the front (*anterior*) walls of both the right and left ventricle as well as the wall of myocardium between the ventricles. (This muscular wall between the ventricles is called the interventricular septum). The other branch — the circumflex artery — brings blood to the left atrium and the left ventricle's back (*posterior*) wall. The two main branches divide and subdivide into many smaller vessels to ensure complete circulation to the left side of the heart.

After supplying the heart's muscular walls with the oxygen and fuel they need, deoxygenated blood returns to the right atrium through several cardiac veins.

But think about this a moment. There could be a problem here! Try this. Squeeze one hand into a tight fist. Then try to push a finger into that fist. You can't! It won't fit if the fist is tightly contracted. Likewise, if your heart is busy squeezing hard — contracting — how can its muscular walls have room to let blood flow through the coronary circulation to bring them the oxygen and fuel they must have to keep working? Well, God is a great engineer. This is the solution He designed: As the heart relaxes during diastole, the pressure in the aorta pushes blood into the coronary arteries to supply the heart. The heart muscle receives most of the oxygen and fuel it needs during the relaxed parts of each heartbeat, enough to keep it going until the next diastole.

Coronary Artery Disease

It is possible that you know someone who has suffered a heart attack. If not, I expect you have at least heard the term "heart attack." A heart attack can be very serious and is often fatal. Every year over 700,000 people in America have a heart attack!

The primary problem that leads to a heart attack is called **coronary artery disease**. You already know what a coronary artery is. Coronary arteries are the arteries that keep the heart's muscular walls supplied with freshly oxygenated blood. Coronary artery disease, abbreviated CAD, occurs when the lining inside a coronary artery becomes thick. As the lining thickens, the channel inside the artery becomes smaller and smaller. Less and less blood is able to squeeze through the narrowing opening. Severe narrowing is called a "blockage."

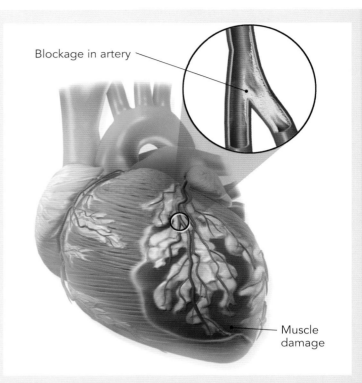

Blockage in artery

Muscle damage

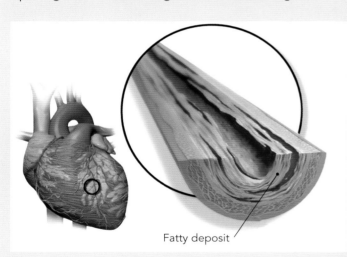

Fatty deposit

Eventually, the blood flowing through this narrowed artery cannot adequately supply the needs of the myocardium. The situation where adequate oxygen is not delivered to the heart muscle is called **myocardial ischemia**. Coronary artery disease can involve a single "blockage" in only one coronary artery or several blockages in multiple coronary arteries. Obviously, the more blocked arteries, the more serious the situation.

Myocardial ischemia is not the same thing as a heart

attack, but it can lead to one. There are degrees of myocardial ischemia. Some people with myocardial ischemia experience episodes of **angina pectoris**, which literally means "strangled chest." A person with angina pectoris has episodes of chest pain, usually described as a tightness or a burning sensation in the chest. Some feel like their chest is in a vise. Often the pain radiates to the left arm, neck, or jaw. Angina pectoris can occur with activity (so-called "stable" angina) or at rest ("unstable" angina). The underlying problem is that due to restriction of blood flow. the heart muscle does not get adequate oxygen to meet its needs, thus resulting in chest pain. However, with angina alone the situation is intermittent, and there is no permanent damage to the heart muscle.

As coronary artery disease worsens, there is increasing danger of myocardial infarction (often called an "MI"). This is commonly known as a heart "attack." Here the disease in the coronary artery (or arteries) has progressed to the point that the myocardium can no longer get the amount of oxygen it needs, and some of the heart muscle dies. Logical, isn't it? If an artery that takes oxygen to a certain part of the heart becomes blocked, then the muscle tissue in that part of the heart is at risk of death. Myocardial infarctions can range from relatively mild to fatal. The severity depends on how much myocardium is damaged and how efficiently the remaining heart muscle functions.

Treatment for coronary artery disease depends on its severity. If it is very mild, a patient may be treated with simple things like exercise, medication, and changes in diet. For more serious blockages, patients may undergo a procedure to open or to by-pass the blockage in order to improve blood flow to the heart.

There are two main sorts of procedures used to deal with a coronary artery blockage. One is called **coronary angioplasty**. (By the way, the author of this book has undergone this procedure.) Here, using special dye and a type of x-ray called fluoroscopy, a tiny wire is threaded through the blockage and a balloon is inflated to open up the artery. Most often, a small mesh device, called a stent, is then put in place in the coronary artery to help keep it open.

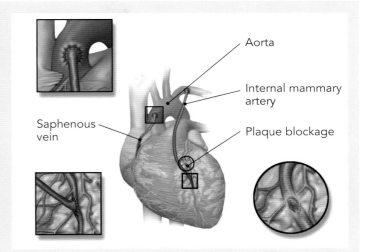

Aorta

Internal mammary artery

Saphenous vein

Plaque blockage

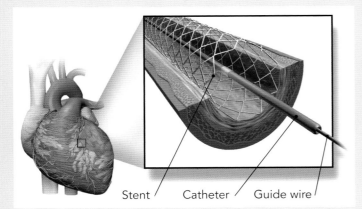

Stent   Catheter   Guide wire

In the most severe cases of coronary artery disease, **coronary artery bypass surgery** is done to route blood around a blockage. In bypass surgery, a section of a vein from the person's arm or leg is removed and used as a bypass graft. One end of the vein is attached to the aorta, and the other end is attached to the diseased coronary artery at a point past the blockage. Thus, the blockage is effectively "bypassed," and blood flow is restored to the heart muscle at risk for damage.

Coronary artery disease is a type of **cardiovascular disease**, a term that includes heart attacks and strokes and other diseases of the heart and blood vessels. Cardiovascular disease is the world's leading cause of death. Heart attacks are the leading cause of death in the United States.

Who is most likely to have a heart attack? Some people are at greater risk than others. A **risk factor** is something that puts a person at greater risk of suffering a particular thing than other people. Some risk factors are beyond a person's control. However, there are some things you can do to lower the risk of ever having a heart attack. There are many risk factors that can lead to heart disease. These include (but are not limited to) smoking, a lack of exercise, obesity, poor diet (especially diets high in fats), high cholesterol, diabetes, and high blood pressure.

We need to take all the steps we can to take good care of our hearts. So make a lifelong practice of getting plenty of exercise (and, no, video games are not exercise), maintain a healthy weight, get in the habit of primarily eating nutritious foods (I'm not saying don't eat hot fudge sundaes, I'm just saying don't make a regular habit of them), and never, ever . . . let me say it again . . . never, EVER, start smoking!

Now is the time to learn a heart healthy lifestyle!

Why the Heart Beats

As we mentioned earlier, cardiac muscle is involuntary. This means you don't have to think about your heart beating. It happens all on its own. Unlike skeletal muscle, you have no conscious control over the contraction of cardiac muscle. For example, you can willfully make skeletal muscle move . . . reaching for a glass or throwing a ball. However, you cannot will your heart to beat.

So what makes the heart beat? I'm glad you asked!

It turns out that just beating isn't enough. Not only must the heart beat (and even be able to speed up when you are running), but both sides must beat simultaneously. Remember, the heart is really two pumps. How does it get the timing right so that both sides pump simultaneously? The answer is electrical. Your heart has a built-in system to produce an electrical signal that triggers the heart muscle in each pump to beat . . . and to do it over and over and over again.

Let's take some time to explore this incredible design.

Most of the heart consists of cardiac muscle cells. The vast majority of these muscle cells are in the business of contracting. They are responsible for the pumping action of the heart. However, about 1 percent of these cells have a very special property and are not primarily involved in heart contraction. These special cells are the ones that *stimulate* the contractions! These cells have the ability to spontaneously generate an electrical signal all on their own. These are called *autorhythmic* ("self-rhythm") cells. They repeatedly produce electrical signals that stimulate the heart to contract.

These autorhythmic cells generate electrical impulses without any outside stimulus from the nervous system. Even if all nerve fibers to the heart were severed, the heart would continue to beat. For

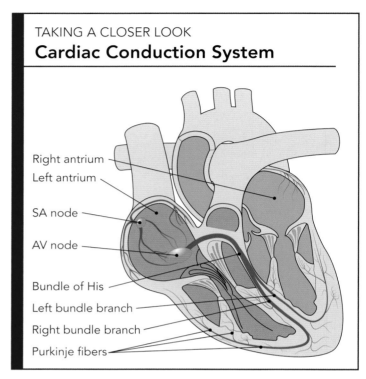

TAKING A CLOSER LOOK
Cardiac Conduction System

Right antrium
Left antrium
SA node
AV node
Bundle of His
Left bundle branch
Right bundle branch
Purkinje fibers

example, hearts removed from a body to be transplanted continue to beat for several hours, even though all nerve fibers to the heart have been cut. (This does not mean that the nervous system is not important. Nervous system input can play an important role in controlling the heart *rate* as we will see.)

These autorhythmic cells have two important jobs. First, they function as the *pacemaker* for the heart. That is, they establish and maintain the basic rhythm of the heart. They trigger the start of each and every heartbeat. They set the pace! Second, they are lined up to form a pathway that helps move the electric signals through the heart from muscle cell to muscle cell in a very orderly fashion.

The cardiac conduction system is also called the *intrinsic conduction system*. *Intrinsic* means this conduction system is completely contained within the heart; it does not bring in messages from outside the heart. This intricate network of rhythm-generating cells is designed to distribute signals to the cardiac muscle in an orderly way to ensure that the heart contracts in a coordinated manner. If the heart's chambers did not coordinate their squeezing action, chambers would start squeezing before they filled. Furthermore, just as a toothpaste tube squeezed near the top traps toothpaste in the bottom of the tube, so a heart that doesn't squeeze in a coordinated manner would not empty blood very well. Let's take a closer look at the way the electrical system of the heart is designed to avoid this sort of problem.

The Cardiac Conduction System

The cardiac conduction system (or intrinsic conduction system) has two "nodes" that set the pace of the heartbeat. The first node to fire signals the beginning of a heartbeat. This pacesetter is the *sinoatrial node*, also called the *SA node*. The SA node is a small group of cells located in the upper portion of the right atrium's wall, near the entrance of the superior vena cava. The SA node is the heart's main pacemaker. The SA node initiates each electrical *impulse* that stimulates the heart to contract. On average, the SA node generates an impulse 72 times a minute. The SA node generates impulses faster than the other pacemaking node. Therefore, under normal circumstances, the SA node controls the heart rate. For that reason, the basic rhythm of the heart is called *sinus rhythm*.

Once generated, the impulse from the SA node travels through the muscle cells themselves. The impulse spreads throughout both atria causing them to contract. Atrial contraction squeezes the blood from each atrium into the ventricles.

At the end of its journey through the atria, the electrical impulse produced by the SA node reaches another group of cells called the *atrioventricular node* (AV node). The AV node is located in the wall (or *septum*) between the right and left atria, just above the tricuspid valve. It is the job of the AV node to send the electrical signal on to the ventricles. That signal makes the ventricles contract. (If, however, the SA node fails for some reason, the AV node can act as a backup system and stimulate the heart to beat.)

Do you see a problem here?

These electrical impulses travel very rapidly. What would happen if the atria and the ventricles all contracted at the same time? The atria would not be able to squeeze their blood into the ventricles because the ventricles would be contracting too. And without getting re-filled with blood from the atria, the ventricles would soon have no more blood to pump out to the body and the lungs. The entire heart would stop pumping blood. Not a good situation at all, right? The beating of the heart must be coordinated, so that the atria both contract before the ventricles do.

God has designed the cardiac conduction system to avoid this problem. When the SA node "fires," both

How Fast?

As we examined the cardiac conduction system, we saw that the SA node is the primary pacemaker of the heart. The SA node beats at an average rate of 72 beats a minute.

Are there other pacemaker locations in the heart? As it turns out, there are.

If the SA node ceased to function (say, as a consequence of disease or aging), the AV node would take over the pacemaker duties. However, the heart rate generated by the AV node is around 50 beats per minute.

And if both the SA and AV nodes stopped working, the Purkinje fibers also have the potential to act as a pacemaker. Purkinje fibers can only generate a heart rate of around 30 beats as minute. This is certainly not ideal, nor is it as efficient as a properly functioning SA node.

God designed two backup systems to keep the heart beating if its chief pacemaker malfunctions.

atria respond almost instantly, and then the AV node "fires." But when the AV node fires, the ventricles do *not* respond immediately. Instead, the AV node's electrical signal is delayed by about 0.1second (that's one-tenth of a second . . . not very long at all . . . but long enough). This delay happens because the cells in the fibers near the AV node do not transmit the electrical impulse as rapidly. (They have fewer *gap junctions*, little gateways between cells, and that slows down the passage of the impulse from cell to cell.) Once through the AV node and these signal-slowing muscle fibers, the signal travels normally (that is, very rapidly) through the remainder of the conduction system.

After leaving the AV node, the signal is carried by the *atrioventricular bundle* (sometimes called the *bundle of His*) into the ventricles. You might be thinking, "Wait a minute, we just saw that this impulse was carried through the atria though the muscle cells themselves. Why can't the signal that passed through the atria reach the ventricles the same way?" Good question. The answer is that the atria and ventricles are separated by the connective tissue that makes up the fibrous skeleton of the heart. This fibrous tissue acts as sort of an insulator that stops the electrical signal from passing directly. The only electrical pathway between the atria and the ventricles is the atrioventricular bundle. Here is

Pacemakers

Even though a healthy heart does have the ability to generate its own conduction signals, there are circumstances when the cardiac conduction system does not function correctly. At times due to aging or illness, the pacemaker center (SA node) may not generate signals rapidly enough to maintain adequate blood pressure. Or perhaps as the consequence of a heart attack, the AV node is damaged and cannot conduct the electrical signals to the ventricles properly.

In many situations like these a patient may require the implantation of a pacemaker. A pacemaker is a small battery-powered device that can help

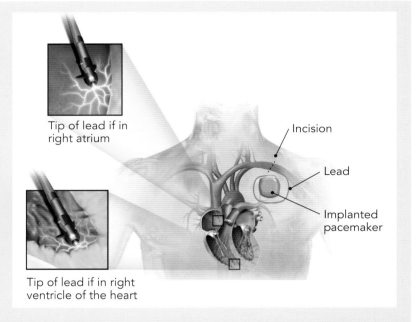

Tip of lead if in right atrium

Incision

Lead

Implanted pacemaker

Tip of lead if in right ventricle of the heart

control a patient's heartbeat. The device is attached to a small electrode that is placed in the heart. An electrical signal is sent from the pacemaker to stimulate the heart to beat.

The simplest style of pacemaker has one electrode that is threaded into the right ventricle (under fluoroscopic guidance). The pacemaker itself is usually placed in a small surgically created pocket under the skin just below the left collarbone. The pacemaker can monitor the patient's heartbeat, and if a beat is not detected within a certain period of time, the pacemaker sends an electrical impulse to stimulate the heart. If a normal heartbeat is detected, then the pacemaker would not fire.

Pacemakers have become more and more sophisticated. These devices can be programmed for a wide range of heart rates. Some pacemakers have multiple electrodes and can pace both the atrium and the ventricle. Other pacemakers sense activity levels and can adjust the patient's heart rate to match.

but one more example of the marvelous design of the heart. Without this electrical barrier it would not be possible to control the pumping action of the heart so precisely.

Very soon after reaching the ventricles, the atrio-ventricular bundle splits into two branches, the *right bundle branch* and the *left bundle branch*. These two bundles proceed down through the *interventricular septum* (the wall between the ventricles) toward the apex of the heart. The right bundle branch delivers the impulse to the right ventricle and the left bundle branch signals the left ventricle. In the septum, the bundle branches also to small branches that penetrate deep into the myocardium of the ventricles. These are called Purkinje fibers. Because the *Purkinje fibers* deliver the electrical signals to their final destination, they are vital for maintaining the heart's smooth, coordinated pumping action. Purkinje fibers cause the heart to contract from the bottom up and not from the top down. Hang on, this is about to make sense. . . .

When the AV node's signal is transmitted, the heart muscle cells in the ventricles do not contract at the same time. What would happen if they did? The blood in the ventricles would get a hard squeeze, but it wouldn't move efficiently toward the aorta and pulmonary artery. To avoid this problem, God has designed the heart's conduction system to start responding to the signal from the apex (the sort of pointy part at the bottom of the heart) and move toward the top of the ventricles. The heart's muscle cells are arranged in a spiral so that they contract and efficiently push the blood in the ventricles out, squeezing from the apex upward. So the heart really does squeeze from the bottom up, and that's the most efficient way!

Think of squeezing a tube of toothpaste. Is it better to squeeze it from the top or the bottom?

Remember, the heart's conduction system is designed (1) to set its own pace by generating an electrical impulse and (2) to send that signal to all parts of the heart in a coordinated manner that first triggers the atria to squeeze blood into the ventricles and then causes the ventricles to squeeze that blood out from the bottom to the top. See if you can name the parts of the conduction system in the order an impulse travels through them.

The Electrocardiogram

The electrical impulses transmitted through the heart can be detected on the body's surface. The heart's electrical signals can be measured with an electrocardiograph. The recording that is produced from this is called an *electrocardiogram* (abbreviated ECG or EKG).

To record an ECG, one electrode (called a *limb lead*) is placed on each arm and leg. (This does not hurt.) Then six other electrodes are placed across the front of the chest. These are the *chest leads*. Multiple

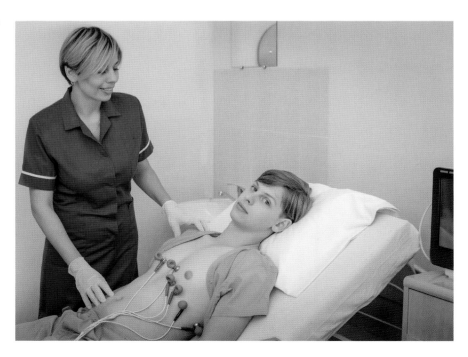

Getting an Electrocardiogram

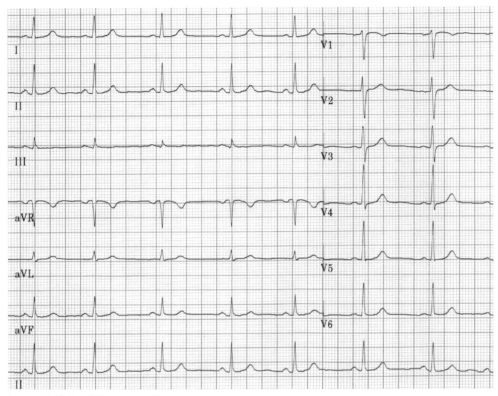

Normal 12 lead Electrocardiogram

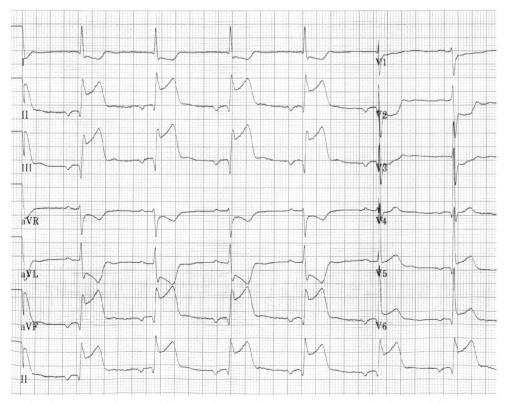

12 lead electrocardiogram of patient having a heart attack. Note the distinct differences from the normal EKG above.

leads are necessary in order to measure the electrical signals from many different positions relative to the heart. The electrocardiograph machine amplifies the signals obtained by the various electrodes and prints out the patterns as an electrocardiogram.

The ECG tracing is a reflection of the electrical signal being transmitted through the cardiac conduction system. As your eyes move from left to right along the tracing, you are seeing a measurement of the electrical signal as it signals each part of the heart in turn. The ECG shows us the electrical signal that instructs the heart to beat and reveals how well that signal travels through the heart, but it does not actually show the heart's response to that signal — the squeezing of the muscle. Other techniques, such as the *echocardiogram*, show the actual beating of the heart.

The first major wave seen on the ECG is called the *P wave*. The P wave reflects the electrical signal that begins the domino effect that ultimately makes the heart beat one time. The P wave reflects the movement of the electrical impulse from the SA node through the myocardium of the atria. About 0.1 second after the P wave begins, the atria contract. The flat segment between the P

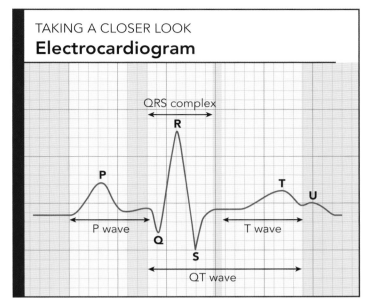

TAKING A CLOSER LOOK
Electrocardiogram

QRS complex
R
P
T
U
P wave
Q
T wave
S
QT wave

become one of the most important tools in modern medicine. Damaged cardiac muscle, for instance, might not transmit the electrical signal properly, and this can be revealed in the ECG. ECGs can be particularly helpful in diagnosing coronary artery disease and cardiac rhythm disorders.

Cardiac Output

To more completely understand how the heart works, there is another concept you must understand. This is known as cardiac output.

Cardiac output (CO) is the amount of blood pumped by the heart in one minute. Cardiac output can vary from minute to minute. For example, when you are running, your leg muscles need more oxygen, right? Of course they do. So what do you think happens to the output of the heart when these muscles need more oxygen? It increases!

When you are asleep, your leg muscles need less oxygen, right? So what happens to the heart output when less oxygen is needed? It is not as high.

Cardiac output is the product of two things: the heart rate (HR) and the stroke volume (SV). *Heart rate* means just what it says, the rate of the heart in beats per minute. *Stroke volume* is the amount (volume) of blood pumped with each heartbeat.

The relationship can be shown this way:

$$CO = HR \times SV$$

So let's calculate an average cardiac output. If the average heart rate is 72 beats per minute, and the stroke volume is 70mL, then

$$CO = 72 \text{ beats/minute} \times 70mL/beat$$
$$CO = 5040mL/minute$$
$$CO = 5.04 \text{ liters/minute}$$
$$(CO = 1.33 \text{ gallons/minute})$$

wave and the beginning of the QRS represents the time after the signal has passed through the atria and is being delayed in the AV node. Remember, it is this delay at the AV node that gives the atria time to squeeze their blood into the ventricles before they contract.

The second large wave seen in a typical ECG is called the *QRS complex*. During the time reflected in the QRS complex the electrical impulse is moving through the ventricles. The QRS complex has a complicated appearance due to the paths that the electrical impulses travel as they move through the ventricular myocardium. This is the time when the ventricles contract. The QRS lasts about 0.1 second.

The last wave in an ECG is the *T wave*. During this time, the ventricle is starting to relax. The ventricles are preparing to receive the next electrical impulse. The duration of the T wave is about 0.16 second, and during this time the electrical system of the heart resets itself in preparation for the next heartbeat.

Then the process begins again.

By understanding the pattern and timing of normal ECGs, doctors can use abnormal ECG patterns to help diagnose and treat patients. In fact, ECGs have

This is a typical cardiac output for an adult at rest.

There are two ways that the cardiac output increases — either the heart rate increases or the stroke volume increases. As you are aware, with exercise, the heart rate increases. You've probably felt your heart beating very fast at the end of a sprint. What you may not realize is that with exercise, your heart's stroke volume — the amount of blood pumped out with each beat — can also increase. If, while running, your heart rate goes to 110 beats per minute and the stroke volume increases to 100 mL (3.4 ounces) per minute, what is the cardiac output?

$$CO = 110 \text{ beats/minute x } 100 \text{ mL/beat}$$
$$CO = 11,000 \text{mL/minute}$$
$$CO = 11 \text{ liters/minute}$$
$$(CO = 2.9 \text{ gallons/minute})$$

So we see that with only mild increases in heart rate and stroke volume, the cardiac output more than doubles! Soon we'll see how the body can let the heart know that it must pump out more blood — that is, that it must increase its cardiac output.

Echocardiogram

An echocardiogram is an ultrasound of the heart. Whereas the EKG evaluates the heart's function by measuring electrical conduction, an echocardiogram uses sound waves to see inside the heart. Using a *transducer* placed on the patient's chest, sound waves are painlessly bounced off various parts of the heart. The resulting pictures show the heart's shape, its walls, valves, and even the blood flowing through its chambers.

By using sound waves to see inside the heart and make measurements, doctors can determine if the heart is working normally or not. Do the walls move properly? Are they too thick? Is the heart enlarged? Do the valves close completely, or does blood leak back through them? How much blood do the heart's chambers pump out with each squeeze? The heart's ejection fraction, a valuable way to assess how well it is pumping, can be calculated based on information from the echocardiogram.

Here you can see samples of echocardiographic images.

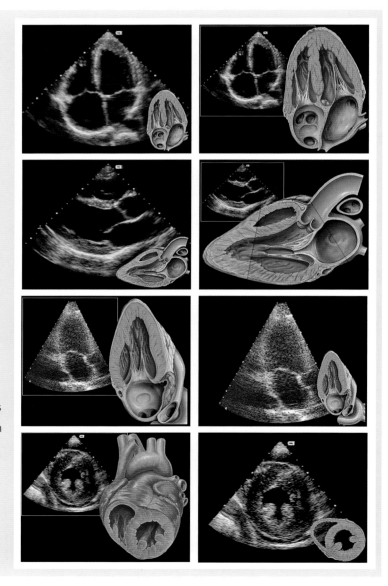

Cardiac Reserve

Some people's hearts are able to increase their cardiac output more than others. A healthy person who runs regularly, for instance, may be able to increase his or her cardiac output much more than a person with heart disease can. We say their *cardiac reserve* is greater.

Cardiac reserve is the difference between the cardiac output at rest and cardiac output during maximal exertion. The average person's heart can increase its output about five times above its resting output. That would be around 24 liters/minute (6.5 gallons/minute). In a highly trained athlete, the maximum cardiac output during heavy exertion might reach 33 liters/minute (9 gallons/minute), or seven times the resting CO.

Regulation of Stroke Volume

Increasing cardiac output requires an increased heart rate, or increased stroke volume, or both. Let's look at ways the stroke volume can increase.

Stroke volume, remember, is how much blood the heart pumps out during one heartbeat. The heart, no matter how healthy, does not empty itself completely during a beat. There is always some blood left behind. Therefore, stroke volume is the difference between the amount of blood in the left ventricle when it is completely relaxed and the amount of blood remaining in the left ventricle when it has just finished contracting.

The ventricle's time of relaxation and filling is called *diastole*, you recall, so the amount of blood in the ventricle when it is full is known as the *end diastolic volume*. *Systole* is the time of contraction, so the amount of blood left in the ventricle after it contracts is called the *end systolic volume*. We could sum this up like this:

End diastolic volume – End systolic volume = Stroke volume

We've said that the heart can increase its stroke volume in order to supply the body's increased needs, like when you want to run. There are several factors that affect stroke volume, but the two most important are *preload* and *contractility*. Preload depends on how much blood is in the left ventricle before it squeezes. Contractility involves how hard the ventricle squeezes. Let's look at these two things more closely.

Cardiac muscle cells contract most efficiently when they are stretched somewhat before they begin contracting. *Preload* is the amount that cardiac muscle is stretched by the blood in the ventricle before it contracts. The more blood that enters the ventricle, the more its walls are stretched. This stretching helps increase the force of the contraction of the muscle. Imagine blowing up a balloon. The more air you blow into a balloon, the more the balloon stretches. Up to a point, the more the ventricle is stretched (preloaded), the stronger will be its contraction.

Preload depends on the amount of blood that can enter the ventricle before it beats. Let's consider how preload can change. The heart's *rate* can alter its preload. If it beats slowly, there is more time between beats. This allows more time for blood to fill the ventricles and increases stroke volume. The opposite can occur with extremely fast heart rates. A very rapidly beating heart leaves little time between beats to fill the ventricle, and the stroke volume could consequently decrease.

The heart muscle's contractility also helps determine stroke volume. *Contractility* refers to how hard the muscle can contract when it is stretched to a certain point. When you are running, your body can send messages to the heart to increase contractility. Some of the most important chemical messengers in the body are called hormones. *Hormones* travel through the blood stream to deliver their messages to many destinations in the body. The hormones *epinephrine* and *norepinephrine* (also called *adrenaline* and *noradrenaline*) can increase the contractility of cardiac muscle, making the muscle squeeze more forcefully. When the heart squeezes harder, it empties more completely with each beat. Thus, stroke volume increases.

Stress Testing

A heart suffering from coronary artery disease might have sufficient blood circulation to function normally at rest but not when stressed with exercise. Therefore, one of the most common tests performed to detect coronary artery disease is called an exercise test, or a "stress" test.

An exercise stress test is performed by having the patient walk on a treadmill while connected to an EKG monitor. Every few minutes, the speed and incline of the treadmill are increased, thus demanding more work from the patient's heart. (Those patients unable to walk on a treadmill can be tested using vigorous arm exercises or an exercise bicycle.) The test ends when the patient cannot continue or when a specified heart rate is achieved.

During the stress test certain characteristic EKG patterns may suggest the presence of coronary artery disease. Abnormal heart rhythms also commonly develop during the exertion of the stress test. These rhythms are recorded on the EKG tracings for evaluation.

Although primarily thought of as a test to detect disease, stress tests are also useful in other ways. For example, special types of stress tests are sometimes used to evaluate and monitor the conditioning of healthy athletes as a part of their training regimen.

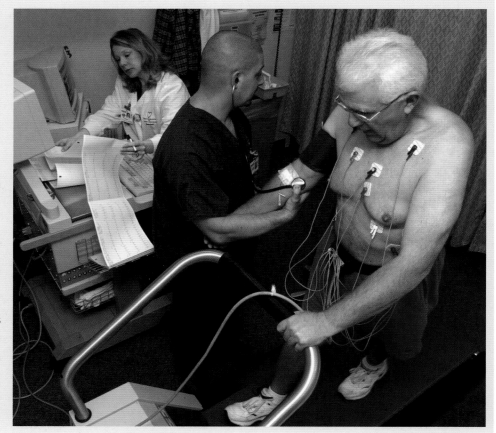

Regulation of Heart Rate

We said the increased cardiac output requires an increased heart rate, or increased stroke volume, or both. Just as there are factors that regulate stroke volume, there are factors that regulate heart rate. The SA node is the heart's main pacemaker. The SA node is part of the heart's *intrinsic* conduction system — a signaling network *inside* the heart — but it responds to input from the nervous system, hormones, and other stimuli.

Everyone knows that our heart beats faster when we are frightened or excited. This increase in heart rate is due in large part to stimulation of the cardiac conduction system by the nervous system. Nerve fibers from the *sympathetic nervous system* release a chemical (norepinephrine) that binds to special receptors on the heart. Sympathetic nerve stimulation causes the SA node to fire more rapidly, and thus increases the heart rate.

The nervous system can also cause the heart rate to decrease. The *parasympathetic nervous system* has effects opposite to the sympathetic nervous system. (We will learn much more about these two divisions of the nervous system in other volumes of *Wonders of the Human Body*.) Parasympathetic fibers release a different chemical (acetylcholine) to slow the speed at which the SA node fires.

The primary pacemaker of the heart, the SA node, fires at an average of 72 beats per minute. However, the SA node is actually "pre-set" at a rate of nearly 100 beats per minute. The SA node fires at a slower average rate because it is reined in the parasympathetic nervous system's input.

Heart rate can be influenced by other things, such as hormones — chemical messengers that travel though the blood stream. One of these — adrenaline (also called epinephrine) — is made by the adrenal glands when you are exercising and when you are frightened. Adrenaline (epinephrine) increases heart rate. Thyroxine, a hormone produced by the thyroid gland, can also increase the heart rate. Fever can increase the heart rate, and an abnormally low body temperature can lower the heart rate.

3

TWO KINDS OF HEARTS

Your heart is designed to beat constantly and to respond to your body's special needs. It pumps in a coordinated fashion to send blood through your lungs to gather oxygen and then on to the rest of your body. If it did not do this, you could not live. The heart can also pump faster or slower or stronger, depending on the signals it receives. Without any conscious thought on your part, it makes all these adjustments. God designed your heart to be dependable and steadfast.

The Bible often refers to a different kind of heart. This sort of heart refers to your character—the emotional, intellectual, and moral being that you are. This kind of heart represents the sort of person you are on the inside.

For as he thinks in his heart, so is he.
"Eat and drink!" he says to you,
But his heart is not with you.
(Proverbs 23:7)

Here we learn that the thoughts of a person's heart reveal the kind of person he or she is.

But the Lord said to Samuel, "Do not look at his appearance or at his physical stature, because I have refused him. For the Lord does not see as man sees; for man looks at the outward appearance, but the Lord looks at the heart."
(1 Samuel 16:7)

The Bible says that while people see what we are like on the outside, the Lord sees the heart. Our true character—that invisible kind of heart—is always visible to the Lord, and He has said in that every person is a sinner.

For all have sinned and fall short of the glory of God.
(Romans 3:23)

God's Word also tells us that we need to truly believe in our hearts in Jesus Christ in order to have salvation from sin. Jesus loves each of us and bought salvation for us when He died on the cross and rose again.

That if you confess with your mouth the Lord Jesus and believe in your heart that God has raised Him from the dead, you will be saved. For with the heart one believes unto righteousness, and with the mouth confession is made unto salvation.
(Romans 10:9-10)

God designed both kinds of hearts—your physical heart that keeps you alive all the days you live on this earth, and the spiritual heart that must trust in Jesus Christ to receive eternal life with Him.

The heart knows, thinks, sees, is wise, speaks, and understands.
Proverbs 15:13–14
Psalm 90:12

The heart is very intentional.
Psalm 27:14
Psalm 119:112

The heart can be hard, stubborn and calloused.
Proverbs 28:14
Ezekiel 36:26

The heart desires, wishes, and envies.
Proverbs 14:30
Psalm 139:23

The heart is emotional.
It loves. It feels things
good and bad.
Matthew 22:37
2 Thessalonians 3:5

The heart can be wicked
and store evil.
Jeremiah 17:9

The heart can be
good, pure and holy.
Psalm 51:10
Proverbs 21:2

4

BLOOD VESSELS

As incredible as the human heart is, without the body's intricate system of blood vessels, it would serve no real purpose. After all, a pump is no good without "pipes" to carry the blood where it's going. The body's vascular system does just that. And more. . .

You see, the body's vascular system is much more than just a collection of tubes that carry blood away from the heart and then back again. These tubes are able to contract and expand in order to control blood pressure and to divert blood to the places where it is most needed. Parts of the vascular system are strong enough to withstand the high pressures the heart generates. Other parts of the system are thin and delicate enough to allow oxygen and nutrients to diffuse across their walls into adjoining tissues.

Not just any old set of tubes is it? Let's take a closer look.

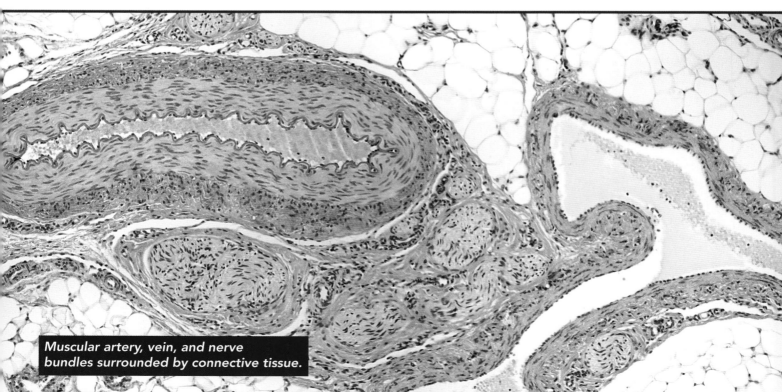

Muscular artery, vein, and nerve bundles surrounded by connective tissue.

Blood Vessels — the Basics

You had probably heard of arteries and veins, even before you began reading this book. We've talked about the difference: veins bring blood toward the heart, and arteries carry blood away from the heart. Now it is time to learn how these vessels branch into other smaller blood vessels and to learn how the differences in the vessels equip them for the important jobs they do.

There are five primary types of blood vessels: arteries, arterioles, veins, venules, and capillaries. Let's review what each type of blood vessel does.

Remember this: *arteries — and their branches — take blood away from the heart.* So it stands to reason that veins and their branches must do the opposite, and that is precisely what they do. *Veins — and their branches — carry blood back to the heart. Capillaries,* which are very small, connect the two. Capillaries get the blood from the arterial system back into the vessels of the venous system.

As we saw earlier, in the systemic circulation (where blood is pumped from the left ventricle into the aorta and out to the body's organs), arteries carry oxygen-rich blood to the tissues and then veins carry the oxygen-poor blood back to the heart. In the pulmo-

nary circulation (where blood is pumped from the right ventricle into the pulmonary artery and out to the lungs), the arteries carry the oxygen-poor blood to the lungs, and the veins carry the oxygen-rich blood back to the heart.

Ultimately, the point of pumping all this blood throughout the body is to deliver oxygen and nutrients to the capillaries where these substances can be made available to the body's tissues. Capillaries are the smallest blood vessels. Their walls are very thin — thin enough to allow the nutrients in the blood to make their way into the surrounding tissues. Waste products produced in the tissues can also cross the

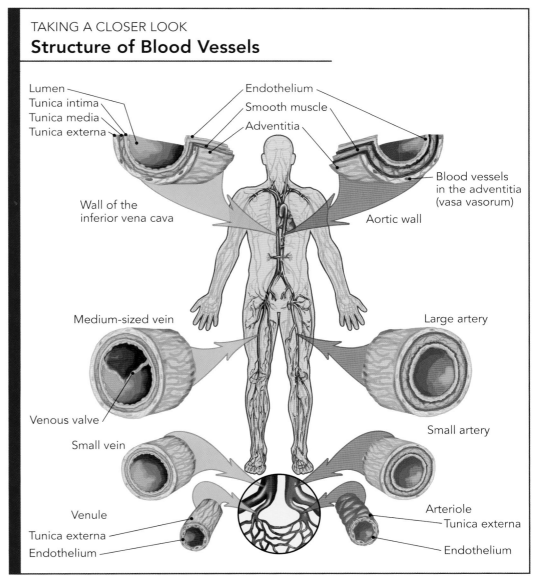

TAKING A CLOSER LOOK
Structure of Blood Vessels

Lumen
Tunica intima
Tunica media
Tunica externa

Endothelium
Smooth muscle
Adventitia

Blood vessels in the adventitia (vasa vasorum)

Wall of the inferior vena cava

Aortic wall

Medium-sized vein

Large artery

Venous valve

Small vein

Small artery

Venule

Arteriole
Tunica externa

Tunica externa
Endothelium

Endothelium

capillary walls to be carried away in the blood. (These waste products include carbon dioxide, which eventually leaves the body when you breathe out. We'll talk more about that later in this book.)

Arteries take blood from the heart, and as they make their way to the various organs and tissues, they branch again and again, getting smaller and smaller as they find their way to all parts of the body. (You can think of this like a tree. Imagine that the trunk of the tree is the aorta. See how the branches get smaller and smaller the farther away they get.) This branching ends when the smallest arteries reach the capillaries. After the blood passes through the capillaries, the veins take over to return the blood to the heart. Here the veins progressively get larger and larger as they approach the heart.

But what about those other vessels, the arterioles and the venules? Where do they fit in? Simple really. *Arterioles* are the smallest arteries, and they lead to the capillaries. Blood travels through the capillaries to the venules. *Venules* are the smallest veins. They carry blood from the capillaries to the larger veins. Like the tributaries of a stream, venules and then veins join together to form larger and larger vessels.

Blood Vessel Structure

Even though arteries and veins have different functions in the vascular system, they do have similarities in their structure. The walls of these blood vessels consist of three layers, each called a "tunic" or *tunica*. These three layers surround the *lumen*. The *lumen* is the open space through which the blood flows.

The innermost layer of a blood vessel is called the *tunica intima*, which means "inner tunic." Tunica intima lines every blood vessel. This lining must be very smooth in order to minimize friction as blood moves through vessels. If the tunica intima were rough, it might trigger blood to clot when it is not supposed to clot. The tunic intima is so smooth because it is mainly made of a smooth layer of tissue called the *endothelium*. Endothelium lines all the blood vessels and the heart itself, where it is the main component of the heart wall's inner layer, called the endocardium, which we discussed earlier. The endothelium lining blood vessels is a continuation of the endocardium of the heart.

The middle of the three layers of a blood vessel is called, not surprisingly, the *tunica media*, which means "middle tunic." It is made of muscular and elastic materials. The smooth muscle and sheets of elastic fibers making up the tunica media are arranged circularly around the blood vessel. This smooth muscle regulates the size of the lumen through which blood flows. When the smooth muscle contracts, the lumen *constricts*, or gets smaller. This is called *vasoconstriction*. (You can see that this word means "vessel getting smaller.") When the smooth muscle relaxes, the lumen *dilates*, or gets bigger (This is called *vasodilation*, meaning "vessel

TAKING A CLOSER LOOK
Structure of a Blood Vessel

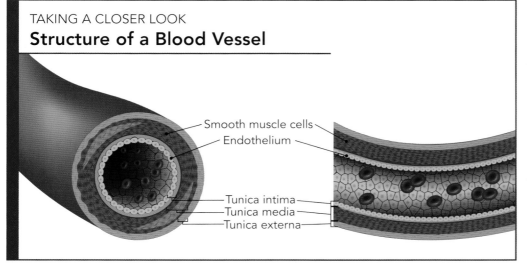

Smooth muscle cells
Endothelium

Tunica intima
Tunica media
Tunica externa

Structure of a Blood Vessel

Elastic artery

- Tunica externa
- Tunica media
- Tunica intima

Muscular artery

- Tunica externa
- Tunica media
- Tunica intima

Arteriole

- Tunica externa
- Tunica media
- Tunica intima

getting bigger.") The elastic sheets enable blood vessels to stretch. The contracting and relaxing of the muscle in the tunica media is controlled by the nervous system as well as by many different chemicals and hormones. More about that later.

The outermost layer of a blood vessel is the *tunica externa*.[1] This layer is made of collagen and elastic fibers. Elastic fibers enable the vessel to stretch and return to its normal size. Collagen supports and protects blood vessels and anchors them to surrounding tissues. Have you ever heard of a disease called *scurvy*? Scurvy is a severe vitamin C deficiency. It was once very common during long sea voyages because fresh fruits and vegetables were generally unavailable. People with scurvy are unable to manufacture collagen properly. This causes many blood vessels to rupture, leading to spongy, bleeding gums, tooth loss, and many severe problems. The collagen in the outer layer of blood vessels is very important!

Arteries

Arteries are the blood vessels that take blood away from the heart. These vessels branch more and more the farther they get from the heart in order to get blood to the entire body. As arteries get smaller they take on different roles, and these new roles are very important. Let's explore the three types of arteries: *elastic arteries*, *muscular arteries*, and *arterioles*.

Elastic arteries are the arteries that are closest to the heart. These include the aorta and the pulmonary artery along with the largest of the arteries that branch from them. Elastic arteries are the largest arteries in the body. They have a lot of elastic fibers in their walls, so they are very "stretchy." Elastic stretches and returns to its normal size. Because of their great elasticity, these large elastic arteries keep pushing the blood forward during the time the ventricles are relaxing. When the left ventricle contracts, it pushes blood under high pressure into the elastic arteries. This pressure stretches the elastic arteries. Then, when the ventricle relaxes, the elastic arteries recoil and keep blood flowing forward.

Muscular arteries are smaller than elastic arteries. The tunica media in muscular arteries is mainly made of smooth muscle and has fewer elastic fibers. Muscular arteries can contract to decrease the flow of blood to certain organs, diverting it to other places. When the muscle relaxes again, the lumen of the vessel is fully open. Having this ability allows the muscular arteries to regulate the amount of blood that is delivered to different parts of the body at any given time. For example, these arteries might help direct more blood flow to your leg muscles if you are running. On the other hand, if you were sitting outside on a cold day watching your favorite team play, muscular arteries might constrict and direct

---

1   It is also at times called the *tunica adventitia*.

blood away from your skin and certain muscles to help conserve your body heat.

The smallest arteries of all are the arterioles. The walls of arterioles are mainly composed of smooth muscle with very little elastic tissue. The arterioles lead into the capillaries. When arterioles contract, the capillaries "downstream" receive very little blood flow. When the arterioles relax, the capillaries "downstream" receive more blood. In this fashion, the arterioles are important in helping regulate the precise delivery of blood to specific tissues.

Capillaries

Capillaries are the smallest blood vessels. They can be found near practically every cell in the body. Capillaries spread throughout tissues. The more capillaries in a tissue, the better it can be supplied with water, oxygen, and nutrients. The brain and kidneys require a lot of energy, and they are supplied with more capillaries than tendons, for instance, which have a lower energy requirement.

Capillaries have a structure that is very different from that of arteries and veins. As you have seen, arteries and veins have walls composed of three layers ("tunics"), and the inner tunic of each is composed of endothelium. The wall of a capillary, however, consists of only a single layer of endothelial cells. This arrangement makes the capillary ideally suited for its purpose, namely, delivering vital substances to the cells surrounding them. Because a capillary wall is so thin, oxygen, water, and nutrients can easily move across it. These substances need only make their way across one cell rather than having to cross all three layers as they would in a larger blood vessel. Because capillaries branch so extensively in tissues, they provide lots of surface area to allow nutrients to quickly move into tissues.

To give you an idea of how small a capillary really is, consider this. The lumen of a capillary is so narrow that red blood cells must pass through single file! (Now that's small!) However, this is still one more example of the incredible design of the body. This single-file passage of the red blood cells through the capillaries may seem inefficient, but it actually allows more contact between each red blood cell and the capillary wall. Thanks to this contact, oxygen moves quickly from the red blood cell through the capillary wall and into the surrounding tissue. See, it wasn't an accident at all.

Veins

After passing through the capillaries, the blood begins its journey back to the heart. This journey begins as the blood from the capillaries drain into small vessels called venules. Think of venules as the first step of the venous system. Venules merge as they get farther away from the capillaries. Eventually they form veins.

Venules are somewhat porous, although not as porous as capillaries. Interestingly, white blood cells are able to leave the bloodstream and enter the tissues through the walls of venules. White blood cells help the body fight infection.

As venules continue to merge, they form veins. Veins continue to merge,

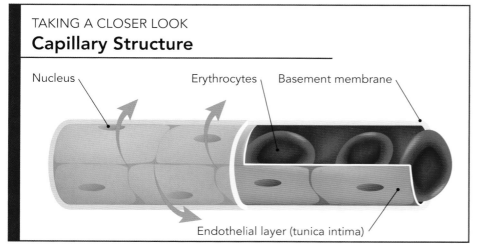

TAKING A CLOSER LOOK
Capillary Structure

Nucleus Erythrocytes Basement membrane

Endothelial layer (tunica intima)

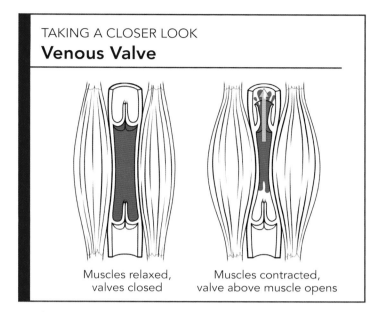

Muscles relaxed, valves closed

Muscles contracted, valve above muscle opens

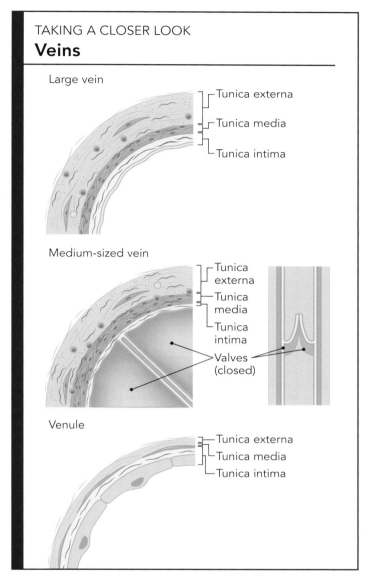

Large vein — Tunica externa, Tunica media, Tunica intima

Medium-sized vein — Tunica externa, Tunica media, Tunica intima, Valves (closed)

Venule — Tunica externa, Tunica media, Tunica intima

coalescing into larger and larger veins as they get closer to the heart.

Veins have three layers as mentioned previously. Their walls are generally thinner than the walls of arteries. Consequently, the lumens of veins are larger than arteries of comparable size.

The primary function of veins is to return blood to the heart. Doesn't sound like too difficult a job, right? Well, it's not as easy as you might think.

You see, arterial blood is pumped out to the body at a high pressure. However, after passing through the capillaries, the pressure is much lower. So it's not as easy getting the blood *back* to the heart.

Fortunately, our Master Designer has this problem solved.

It's easy to imagine how blood pumped to the head and arms gets back to the heart. Gravity can do some of the work, because the blood mostly has to flow down. But what about the blood that has to get back from the legs and other parts of the body below the heart? Blood in those veins must go against gravity to reach the heart. As it turns out, many veins that come from areas of the body below the heart have

small folds of the tunica intima that form *valves*. These valves prevent blood from flowing backward in the veins.

Return blood flow to the heart is also enhanced by the contraction of the muscles in the legs. As we move about, the leg muscles help compress the veins in the legs. This helps push blood back to the heart.

But no matter what part of the venous system we are talking about, more blood is still coming along from the capillaries. Therefore, venous blood is herded along through the venous system, pushed toward the heart by the blood behind it.

5

PHYSIOLOGY OF CIRCULATION

Ultimately, the cardiovascular system is just a pump connected to a set of tubes. The pump pushes the blood out into the tubes. The tubes take the blood to its destinations and return it to the pump. This loop repeats and repeats and repeats. . .

But what controls the pump? What determines how much it pumps? How does it know how hard to pump? How do the pump and tubes fine tune their performance to your body's immediate needs? These are great questions. Let's get some answers.

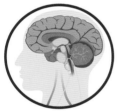  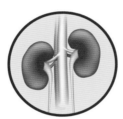 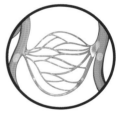

Hemodynamics 101

Have you ever felt your own pulse, had your blood pressure checked, or seen someone have their blood pressure checked by a nurse or a machine at the pharmacy? Most people know the term "blood pressure," even if they are not really sure what it means.

Now we are going to take a closer look at these concepts and help you better understand how the cardiovascular system works. We will start with a few simple ideas.

Your Pulse

Your pulse is a measure of how fast your heart is beating. The heart pushes blood into your arteries every time it beats. You can feel the effect of the blood being repeatedly forced into the arterial system and count it to determine your pulse.

You can feel your pulse at many different places on your body. These are locations where certain arteries run close to the surface of the body. Some of the most common places to check the pulse are the brachial artery (in the bend of the elbow), the radial artery (in the wrist near the base of the thumb), and the *dorsalis pedis* (on the top of the foot). Check the illustration to see many of these locations. If you ever take a first aid course, you may learn to check the pulse by feeling the *carotid artery* in the neck. Many runners also do this. It is *very important* to only check a carotid pulse on one side of the neck. *Never put pressure on both left and right carotid arteries at the same time*, as this can trigger a dangerous reflex in which the heart rate drops.

Pulse rate is recorded in beats per minute. The normal resting pulse rate in an adult is around 70–75 beats per minute, but this can vary. Young children often have faster resting heart rates.

Blood Flow

The amount of blood that flows through the cardiovascular system in a given time period is called *blood flow*. (At times it may be helpful to consider blood flow through a specific blood vessel or an organ. However, for now, let's just look at the system as a whole.) But wait a minute. Haven't we already studied the output of the heart? Indeed, we have. Remember the term *cardiac output* (CO)? For all practical purposes (when talking about the whole system and not just a single organ), blood flow and cardiac output are the same thing. The heart squeezes and the blood flows.

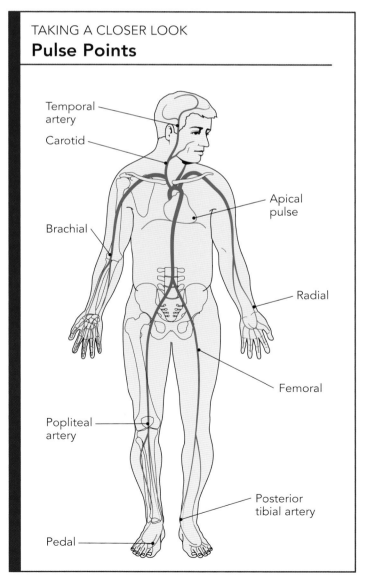

TAKING A CLOSER LOOK
Pulse Points

Temporal artery
Carotid
Apical pulse
Brachial
Radial
Femoral
Popliteal artery
Posterior tibial artery
Pedal

Too Slow? Too Fast?

A heart rate below 60 beats/minute is called *bradycardia*. It is not uncommon for well-conditioned people to have a resting heart rate in this range. However, in certain circumstances a low resting heart rate can be an indicator of heart disease.

A heart rate above 100 beats/minute is called *tachycardia*. It is quite normal for the heart rate to exceed 100 beats/minute with exertion, and a young infant typically has a faster resting heart rate than an older child or adult. However, in an adult, a resting heart rate above 100 beats/minute most often requires further investigation.

Have you ever stopped to think about *why* blood flows? It's very important to know this. In fact, you really can't understand the cardiovascular system until you get this. Ready? Blood flows from areas of high pressure to areas of lower pressure.

Yes, that's pretty much the story. Blood flows from higher pressure to lower pressure.

The heart muscle contracts, generating a high pressure. This high pressure pushes blood into the aorta. The high pressure of the blood being forced into the aorta's lumen stretches it. Then, after the aortic valve closes, the aorta recoils a bit. This elastic recoil maintains a relatively high pressure in the aorta while forcing the blood into other arteries downstream. That pressure pushes the blood on toward the capillaries, then on into the venules and veins. Notice here that the blood flows toward the lower pressures.

Blood Pressure

When blood is pushed into a blood vessel it exerts some degree of force against the wall of the vessel. Blood pressure is simply the pressure of blood inside a vessel.

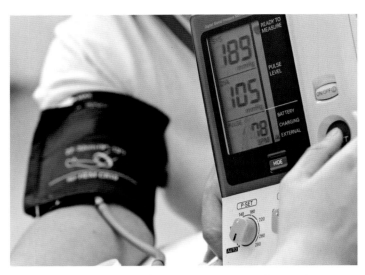

When the left ventricle squeezes (systole) and pushes blood into the arteries, the pressure in the arteries rises. The highest pressure reached in the arterial system at this time is called the *systolic blood pressure* (SBP). The average SBP in a typical healthy adult is 120 mm Hg (blood pressure is measured in millimeters of mercury).

Next, the ventricle relaxes (diastole). Now the walls of the arteries recoil and the pressure decreases as blood is pushed forward. The lowest pressure reached is called the *diastolic blood pressure* (DBP). The average DBP in a healthy adult is 80 mm Hg.

When a blood pressure reading is taken, it is most often recorded like this: 120/80 or 136/74 or 118/62, etc. Those are strange fractions, right? Well, they are not fractions. This is just the way that blood pressures have come to be displayed. The top number is the systolic pressure. The bottom number is the diastolic pressure. No fractions involved.

Pulse Pressure

The difference between the systolic and diastolic blood pressure is called the *pulse pressure*. In our "average" adult with a blood pressure of 120/80, the pulse pressure is around 40 mm Hg (120 mm Hg - 80 mm Hg). The pulse pressure is greatest in the large arteries near the heart, and it decreases as you get farther and farther from the heart. By the time blood gets to the capillaries, the pulse pressure disappears, but the blood keeps moving.

We mentioned above that "pulse" is a measure of how fast the heart beats. Have you ever felt your pulse? If you have, then you have felt the effect of the pulse pressure. You see, the pulse pressure results in a throbbing sensation in an artery that can be felt at certain points along the paths of arteries that run near the surface of the body.

So if the arterial pressure is higher with systole and lower in diastole, which pressure is important? If the pressures just go up and down all the time, how can we make sense of all this? Actually, there is an easy way to calculate an average pressure, and its called the *mean arterial pressure* (MAP).

$$MAP = DBP + pulse\ pressure/3$$

Let's use our typical adult and make the calculation:

$$MAP = 80\ mm\ Hg + (40\ mm\ Hg/3)$$

$$MAP = 80\ mm\ Hg + 13\ mm\ Hg$$

$$MAP = 93\ mm\ Hg$$

Here is the key. The MAP is the pressure that pushes the blood through the blood vessels. It is greatest near the heart and gradually decreases as the distance from the heart increases. For example, near the end of the capillaries, the MAP has decreased to 15-20 mm Hg.

Hemodynamics 102

So we know more about blood flow and pulse and blood pressure. How can these things adjust to changes in a person's activity? Or illness? Don't these things change a lot in both sickness and health? What controls those changes?

The body functions best when it operates under optimal conditions. The body functions best when the blood pressure is just right and the blood sugar level is just right and the body temperature is just right and the oxygen level is just right. The body's many control systems exist to try and keep things just right. Having these things in the right balance is called *homeostasis*. The same control systems that God designed to maintain the body's homeostasis also enable the body to adjust to changes. Let's consider the controls that keep the cardiovascular

Taking your pulse is easy. Using light pressure with your index finger, locate the throbbing sensation on the inner portion of the wrist just below the base of the thumb. This is your radial pulse.
Using a watch or a timer that indicates seconds, count the number of beats in 15 seconds. Then, multiply that number by four. That is your heart rate in beats per minute!

system in balance and enable it to adjust to meet the body's changing needs from moment to moment.

Cardiovascular Center

In the brain — specifically, in the *medulla oblongata* — is the cardiovascular center. The cardiovascular center is the part of the nervous system that oversees regulation of the heart and blood vessels. This region of the brain gets input from multiple sources in the body and then responds by sending nerve signals to the heart and/or the blood vessels.

The cardiovascular center gets input from higher regions of the brain, such as the *cerebral cortex*, where our conscious thinking takes place, as well as the parts of the brain that handle our emotions. The cardiovascular center also processes input from special pressure receptors in the arteries. After processing these various inputs, the cardiovascular center sends the appropriate signal to the heart and blood vessels in various parts of the body to achieve the desired response.

What sort of messages might the cardiovascular center send? Well, a nerve signal might be sent to a particular arteriole to relax and dilate slightly in order to decrease the mean (average) arterial pressure. Or a signal could be sent to constrict slightly and increase the arterial pressure. These changes could make blood pressure drop or rise slightly, or return it to normal. If you are anxious about something, a signal from the cerebral cortex to the cardiovascular center also might result in your heart rate increasing. Signals might be sent to certain arterioles to constrict and decrease blood flow to certain organs while at the same time providing increased blood supply to other organs. For instance, if you need to run away in an emergency soon after you eat, blood that was busy supplying your digestive system will be diverted away from your stomach and sent instead to your legs. Digestion will just have to slow down and wait until you are through running to safety!

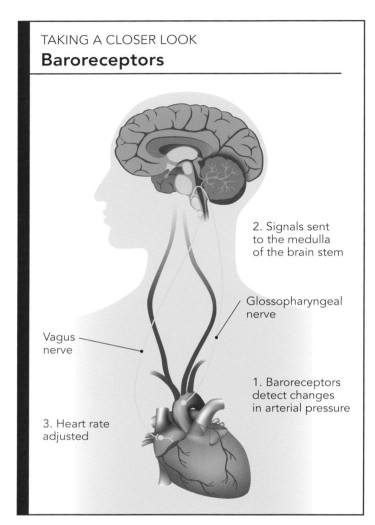

TAKING A CLOSER LOOK
Barometers

2. Signals sent to the medulla of the brain stem

Glossopharyngeal nerve

Vagus nerve

1. Baroreceptors detect changes in arterial pressure

3. Heart rate adjusted

Now we will examine a few of the sensors that constantly send information to the cardiovascular center in more detail.

Baroreceptors

Have you ever heard of a barometer or barometric pressure? These terms refer to measurement of the air pressure. Barometric pressure affects weather. The prefix *baro* means "pressure." Well, your body has its own pressure sensors inside your blood vessels.

Located in the aorta and several of the larger arteries in the upper body are pressure-sensitive receptors known as *baroreceptors*. These receptors are necessary for the minute-to-minute control of blood pressure. And remember, we said that the body works best at optimal conditions. The goal of the cardiovascular center is to regulate blood pressure to keep it in the normal range while allowing your body to do all the things it needs to do.

When blood pressure increases, baroreceptors are stretched. This stretching causes the receptors to send more nerve impulses to the brain. This in turn results in the cardiovascular center signaling the arterioles to dilate. Thus, this nerve reflex ultimately causes a decrease in blood pressure, returning the pressure to normal. Stimulation of baroreceptors also can slow the heart rate to some degree and decrease the contractility of the heart. These changes obviously lower the cardiac output, which also lowers the blood pressure. Lower cardiac output and vasodilation lower the blood pressure to appropriate levels.

In the opposite situation, when the blood pressure is low, the baroreceptors are not being stretched much and therefore send fewer signals to the brain. As a result, the cardiovascular center stimulates arterioles to constrict, increasing blood pressure back to normal. Additionally, the cardiovascular center causes an increase in heart rate and myocardial contractility, and with these there is an increase in cardiac output. Higher cardiac output and vasoconstriction raise the blood pressure to appropriate levels.

Hormones and Blood Pressure

Some hormones have a direct effect on the cardiovascular system. Remember that hormones are chemical messengers that travel through the blood to reach many parts of the body.

Stimulation of the adrenal glands by the nervous system — perhaps due to fear, excitement, or anger — can cause the release of the hormones epinephrine (adrenaline) and norepinephrine (noradrenaline). As we have seen previously, these hormones can cause an increase in both heart rate and myocardial contractility, and consequently cardiac output may increase. The blood pressure can go up when more blood is moved more forcefully out of the left ventricle.

The kidneys have a great deal of control over blood pressure. When blood pressure decreases, blood flow to the kidneys is also decreased. When the kidneys detect the low blood flow, cells in the kidney secrete the hormone renin. Renin activates a hormone known as angiotensin

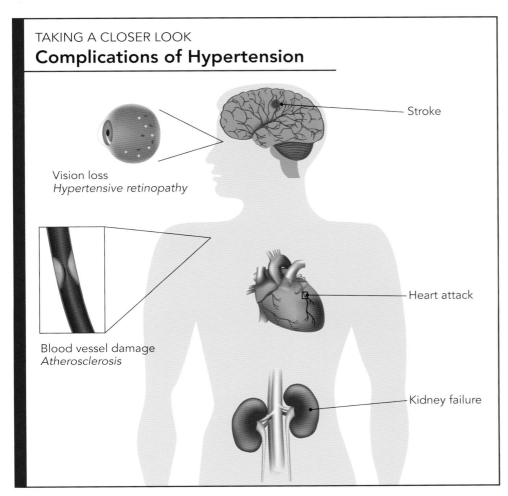

TAKING A CLOSER LOOK
Complications of Hypertension

Stroke

Vision loss
Hypertensive retinopathy

Blood vessel damage
Atherosclerosis

Heart attack

Kidney failure

II. Angiotensin II causes vasoconstriction and raises blood pressure.

Hypertension

The average blood pressure in a healthy adult is 120/80. However, blood pressure varies throughout the day, reacting to the various stresses we encounter. Blood pressure can increase with emotional stress or heavy exertion, but these situations are very short in duration, and blood pressure quickly returns to the normal range. When a person has a blood pressure that is chronically over 140/90 it is known as hypertension. This is commonly called "high blood pressure."

When the left ventricle squeezes, the pressure inside the ventricle rises. When the pressure in the ventricle becomes greater than the pressure in the aorta, the blood is pushed through the aortic valve and out to the body. However, if a person has hypertension, the pressure in the aorta is higher than normal. In this case, the left ventricle has to generate a higher pressure to push the blood out. As the heart is required to constantly pump against

this higher pressure for many months, the wall of the ventricle thickens. Ultimately, this stress on the ventricle results in damage to the muscular wall of the ventricle and the heart is weakened.

Also, exposure to these abnormally high pressures will cause the walls of arteries to thicken and become less flexible. This can lead to damage not only to the arteries of the heart but also to the blood vessels in the brain and kidneys.

Hypertension is one of the most common medical problems in the world. By some estimates, 25 percent of the world's population has hypertension. It is often called a "silent killer," because people can have the problem for many years before they develop symptoms. The damage to the heart, blood vessels, kidneys, and other organs can slowly progress for years before a person has any symptom to make them aware there is any problem at all. For this reason, one of the primary goals in modern medical practice is to identify patients with hypertension and take all necessary steps to control it.

TAKING A CLOSER LOOK
Hypertension – Damage to the Heart

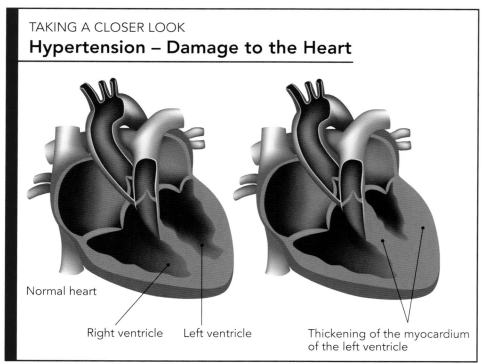

Normal heart

Right ventricle   Left ventricle

Thickening of the myocardium of the left ventricle

Shock

As we have stated from the beginning, the primary purpose of the cardiovascular system is to deliver oxygen and nutrients to the body's tissues. As a general rule, the cardiovascular system does this extremely well (just like it was designed to do). However, we live in a fallen, cursed world, and things don't always work as planned.

There are situations in which the cardiovascular system cannot deliver adequate blood flow to meet the body's needs. This is called *shock*. There are various forms of shock and people in these situations are critically ill. Immediate medical intervention is required in all cases of shock.

The most common type of shock occurs when a person suddenly loses a great deal of blood. This might occur as the result of an accident, for example. Here, the loss of volume is so great that the body cannot generate adequate blood pressure and blood flow. This is called *hypovolemic* ("low volume") shock. The body's cardiovascular center tries to restore normal blood pressure — to restore homeostasis — by causing the heart rate to increase and many arterioles to constrict. When a person is in hypovolemic shock, the body's efforts to maintain homeostasis are not sufficient. The body cannot generate a sufficiently high blood pressure to supply the needs of the brain and other vital organs. Medical help is needed. The primary method of treating hypovolemic shock is by giving the patient blood transfusions and intravenous fluids. This increases the patient's blood volume, giving the cardiovascular system a larger amount of fluid to move around. With increased blood pressure, circulation can better bring needed oxygen and nutrients to the brain and body. Naturally the cause of the blood loss must also be treated!

There are situations where a person has a massive heart attack, and the resulting damage to the heart is so severe that the heart cannot pump adequately. This situation can result in *cardiogenic* shock. In this case the blood volume of the body is normal, but the heart cannot pump the needed oxygen and nutrients to the tissues. Doctors may give the patient medication to try to increase the heart's ability to contract and to decrease the damage to the heart. A patient in shock is also given extra oxygen to breathe in hopes of getting more oxygen into the blood and to the brain, heart, and other vital organs.

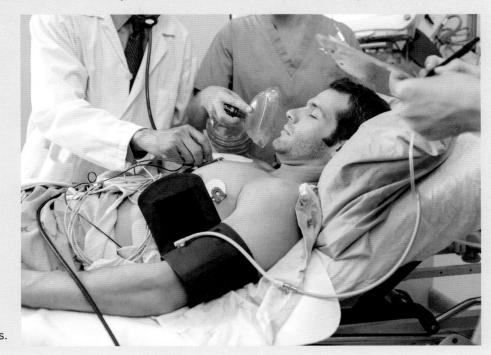

Another form of shock is called *vascular shock*. Vascular shock results from circumstances where blood vessels become too dilated (vasodilation). Here the pumping action of the heart is normal but adequate blood pressures are not obtained because the vasodilation is so extreme. This type of shock can occur during life-threatening infections or severe allergic reactions.

6

THE CIRCULATORY SYSTEM

By this time you should be very familiar with the anatomy and physiology of the heart. You have even learned quite a bit about the structure of blood vessels and how they work. Before we finish our exploration of the cardiovascular system, let's spend a little time on the anatomy of the systemic circulation. (We will examine the pulmonary circulation a little more closely later in this book.)

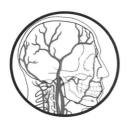 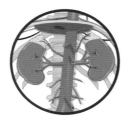 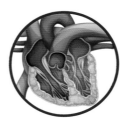 

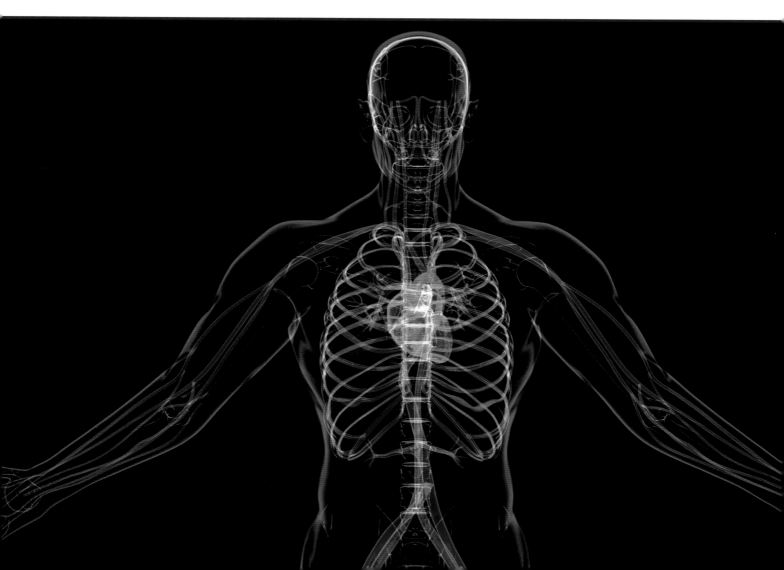

The Systemic Circulation

The systemic circulation consists of the blood vessels that carry blood from the heart to the body's tissues and back again. It begins with the aorta.

The aorta is the largest artery in the body with a diameter of roughly one inch. It is considered to have four portions.

The Aorta

The small section of the aorta when it leaves the heart is called the *ascending aorta*. This small section is noteworthy because the coronary arteries that supply oxygenated blood to the heart muscle begin here. Next, the aorta bends and turns downward. It arches. Therefore, this part of the aorta is called the *aortic arch*. As the aorta proceeds down through the body, it changes names again. The *thoracic aorta* is the portion of the aorta in the thoracic (chest) cavity above the diaphragm, which separates the chest from the abdomen. The *abdominal aorta* is the remaining section of the aorta below the diaphragm. The abdominal aorta is located in the back of the abdomen, near the spine.

TAKING A CLOSER LOOK
The Systemic Circulation

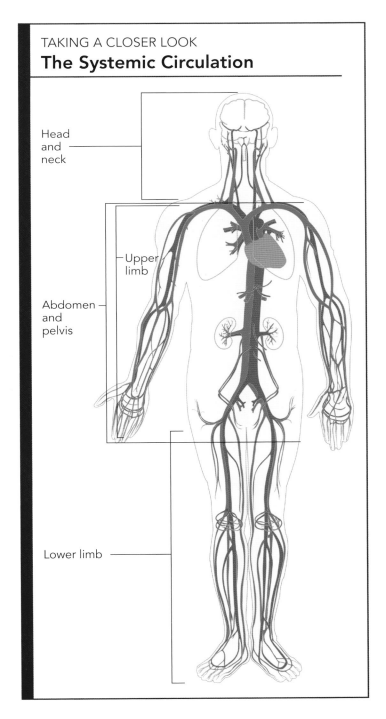

Head and neck

Upper limb

Abdomen and pelvis

Lower limb

TAKING A CLOSER LOOK
The Aorta

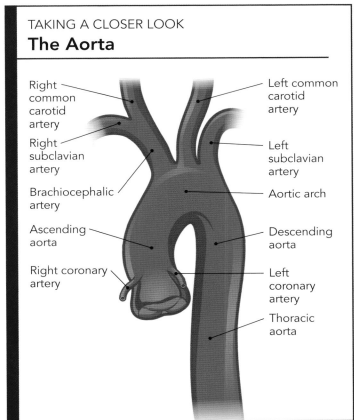

Right common carotid artery

Right subclavian artery

Brachiocephalic artery

Ascending aorta

Right coronary artery

Left common carotid artery

Left subclavian artery

Aortic arch

Descending aorta

Left coronary artery

Thoracic aorta

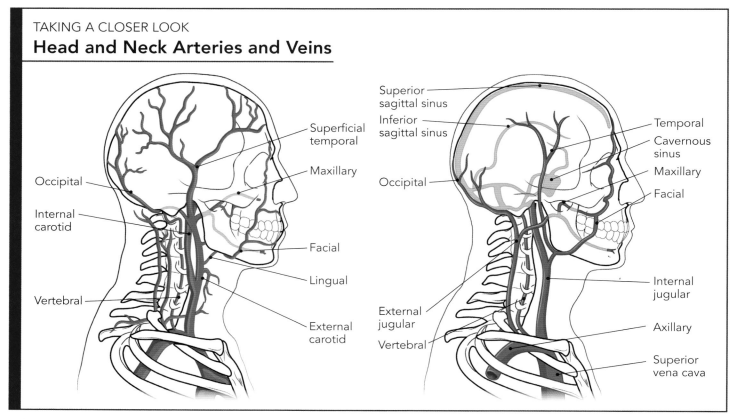

TAKING A CLOSER LOOK
Head and Neck Arteries and Veins

Superficial temporal
Maxillary
Occipital
Internal carotid
Facial
Vertebral
Lingual
External carotid

Superior sagittal sinus
Inferior sagittal sinus
Occipital
External jugular
Vertebral
Temporal
Cavernous sinus
Maxillary
Facial
Internal jugular
Axillary
Superior vena cava

The Head and Neck

As you examine the arch of the aorta, you will see three major arteries — the brachiocephalic trunk, the left common carotid artery, and the left subclavian artery. As you can see from the illustration, soon after it branches from the aorta, the brachiocephalic trunk gives off the right common carotid artery. The common carotid arteries provide blood supply to the head.

The common carotid arteries each soon divide into internal and external branches. The internal carotid arteries provide the primary blood flow to the brain and the eye. The external carotid arteries supply blood to the other tissues in the head.

The venous drainage of the head brings blood back to the heart through the internal and external jugular veins.

Upper Limb

Blood is supplied to the upper limbs via the subclavian arteries. The right subclavian artery branches off the brachiocephalic trunk, but the left subclavian artery comes directly from the aortic arch. Each subclavian artery runs down the arm and changes names according to where in the arm it is located. First it becomes the axillary artery and later the

TAKING A CLOSER LOOK
Arteries of the Brain

Anterior communicating
Middle celebral
Anterior celebral
Internal carotid
Posterior communicating
Basilar
Posterior celebral
Vertebral

brachial artery, in the upper arm. Near the elbow the brachial artery splits into the radial and ulnar arteries which travel down the forearm carrying blood toward the hand.

The venous return is by way of the cephalic, basilic, and brachial veins which ultimately form the subclavian vein.

The final return path from both arms and the head is the superior vena cava, the large veins that drain into the right atrium from above.

TAKING A CLOSER LOOK
Upper Limb Arteries and Veins

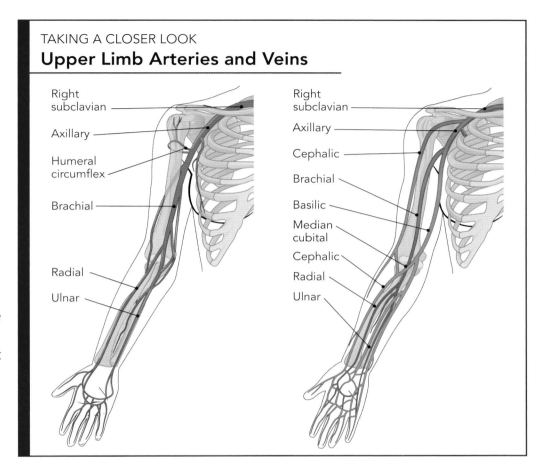

Right subclavian
Axillary
Humeral circumflex
Brachial
Radial
Ulnar

Right subclavian
Axillary
Cephalic
Brachial
Basilic
Median cubital
Cephalic
Radial
Ulnar

TAKING A CLOSER LOOK
Thorax and Abdomen Arteries and Veins

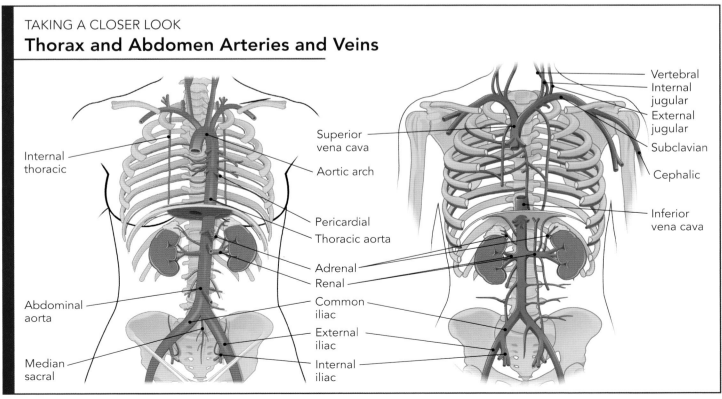

Internal thoracic

Abdominal aorta

Median sacral

Superior vena cava
Aortic arch
Pericardial
Thoracic aorta
Adrenal
Renal
Common iliac
External iliac
Internal iliac

Vertebral
Internal jugular
External jugular
Subclavian
Cephalic
Inferior vena cava

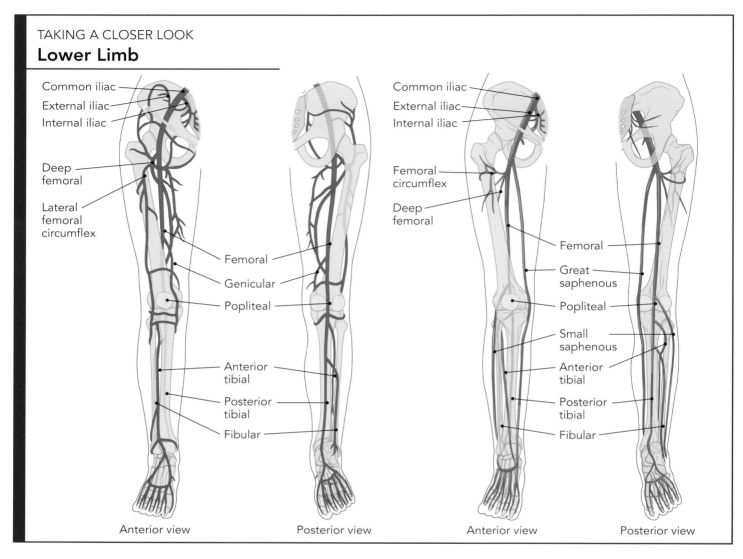

TAKING A CLOSER LOOK
Lower Limb

Common iliac
External iliac
Internal iliac

Deep femoral

Lateral femoral circumflex

Femoral

Genicular

Popliteal

Anterior tibial

Posterior tibial

Fibular

Anterior view

Posterior view

Common iliac
External iliac
Internal iliac

Femoral circumflex

Deep femoral

Femoral

Great saphenous

Popliteal

Small saphenous

Anterior tibial

Posterior tibial

Fibular

Anterior view

Posterior view

Abdomen and Pelvis

The portion of the aorta below the diaphragm is the abdominal aorta. As it courses through the abdomen, several arterial trunks arise from the aorta. These include the celiac trunk, the superior mesenteric artery, and the inferior mesenteric artery. The renal arteries also branch from the aorta.

In the pelvis, the abdominal aorta branches into the right and left common iliac artery.

The venous return from the abdomen and pelvis is via the inferior vena cava. The inferior vena cava is formed by the joining of the two common iliac veins.

Lower Limb

The common iliac arteries supply the lower limbs. The primary arteries in the lower limb are the femoral, the popliteal, and the anterior and posterior tibial arteries.

Venous return from the lower limb is via the tibial, saphenous, and femoral veins.

Your Spiritual Heart

The heart is commonly thought of as the well-spring of our deepest emotions. It seems to pound when we're scared, and soar upward when we're in love. When we are very disappointed or sad, we might say our heart is broken. Perhaps, if a person is particularly enthusiastic about an activity, we might say about them, "John has a real *heart* for playing the piano" or "Mary has a *heart* for that project."

The heart also represents our genuine thoughts and motives. The Bible warns, "The heart is deceitful above all things, and desperately wicked" (Jeremiah 17:9), letting us know how we as sinful people often deceive ourselves. A person can "harden" his heart (Exodus 8:32) like the Egyptian pharaoh in the time of Moses. Or a person can be sorry for his sins: Psalm 51:17 tells us God honors a "broken and a contrite heart," referring to sincere repentance.

So imagine the surprise people felt when William Harvey in 1628 told the world the heart was a pump!

Nonetheless, the heart is a good metaphor for that invisible part of ourselves that thinks and feels and will even live after our physical bodies die. Jesus promises to "dwell in your hearts through faith" (Ephesians 3:17) if you have accepted the salvation He offers. So His presence in your spiritual heart gives you eternal life, and your physical heart must keep doing its job for you to have physical life

But more than anything else, Jesus wants you to love God with all your heart.

Jesus said to him, "You shall love the LORD your God with all your heart, with all your soul, and with all your mind." This is the first and great commandment. (Matthew 22:37–38).

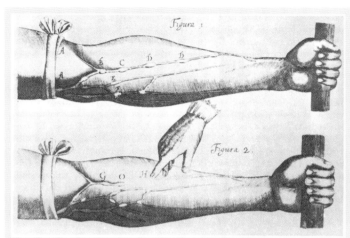

William Harvey (1578-1657) was an English physician who was the first person to describe the circulatory system in detail. He demonstrated that blood flows throughout the body by way of a single system of arteries and veins. This was supported by solid observations and experiments. Before Harvey, most people thought that the arterial and venous systems were separate.

Harvey's famous work on this subject was called *Anatomical Exercise on the Motion of the Heart and Blood in Animals.*

THE RESPIRATORY SYSTEM

It's a fact. In fact, it's a simple fact. We can't live without breathing.

The cells in our bodies need oxygen. Without oxygen, the chemical reactions in our cells that generate energy would quickly shut down. Without energy, the cells would die.

As our cells use oxygen and nutrients to produce energy, carbon dioxide is produced. This carbon dioxide is essentially a waste product. When it is dissolved in liquid, carbon dioxide becomes an acid. Therefore, if carbon dioxide were to remain in the body, it would cause the acid levels in the blood to increase to dangerous levels.

So how do we get oxygen in and carbon dioxide out?
Just take a deep breath and you've got your answer.

And the LORD God formed man of the dust of the ground, and breathed into his nostrils the breath of life; and man became a living being (Genesis 2:7).

Do you know that you really do have holes in your head? They are called sinuses.

You right lung has three lobes, but your left lung only has two. Do you know why?

Did you know that your heart really doesn't stop when you sneeze?

Did you know that there are around 300,000,000 air sacs (alveoli) in EACH of your lungs?

1

BREATHING — NO BIG DEAL?

Ever think about breathing? You probably don't. At least not very often.

It is something that the average person does 14 to 16 times a minute, morning, noon, and night, day in and day out, for a lifetime. Ninety-nine percent of the time, you never give it a thought. It's almost totally automatic.

Yet without breathing, you would die.

The respiratory system provides a means to take in oxygen and get rid of carbon dioxide. But it does so much more. . .

 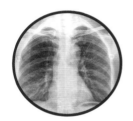  

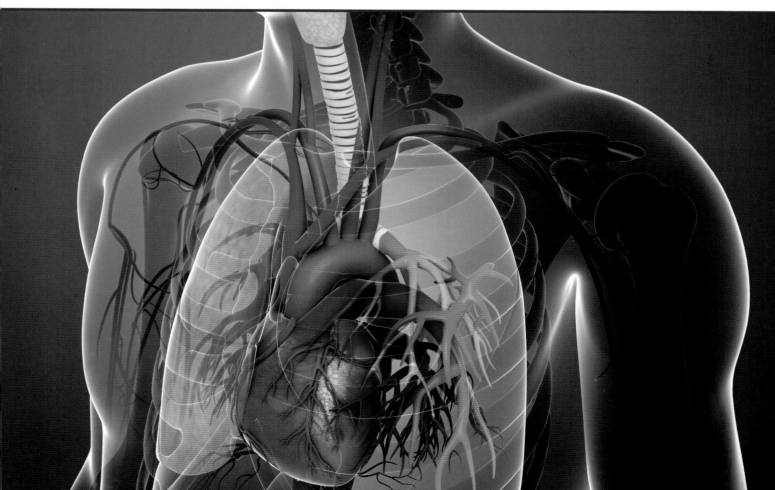

The respiratory system allows us to communicate with others more effectively. When we speak to a friend or shout at a ballgame or laugh at a joke or sing in church, we are relying on our respiratory system. Without it, none of these activities would be possible.

As we will see, the respiratory system also protects us from bad things in our environment. There are lots of bad things in the air we breathe — dust, pollen, and germs. The air we take into our lungs can contain these things. The respiratory system is designed to, at least in some degree, protect us from them.

The respiratory system even protects us from air that is too cold or too dry for comfort. It warms and humidifies the air we breathe even before it reaches our lungs.

Our Creator designed this system pretty well, don't you think?

If you don't think so yet, you will before we're done.

Anatomy of the Respiratory System

As we begin our exploration of the anatomy of the respiratory system, let's look at its parts and what they do. When you breathe in — or *inhale* — air must travel through the respiratory system from top to bottom. And when you breathe out — or *exhale* — air must follow the same path in reverse.

Inhaled air must first travel through the "upper respiratory system." The upper respiratory system is the part above your chest. It consists of the nose, nasal cavity, the sinuses, the pharynx, and the larynx. *Pharynx* — pronounced "fair-inks" — is the anatomical word for "throat." *Larynx* is pronounced "lair'-inks" and rhymes with pharynx. Larynx is the word for your voice box. Your throat is designed to direct air toward your lungs and food and drink toward your stomach. Air passes through your voice box as it enters and leaves your chest, and you are able to use exiting air to generate the sound vibrations of speech.

Inhaled air continues on through the "lower respiratory system." The lower respiratory system contains the trachea,

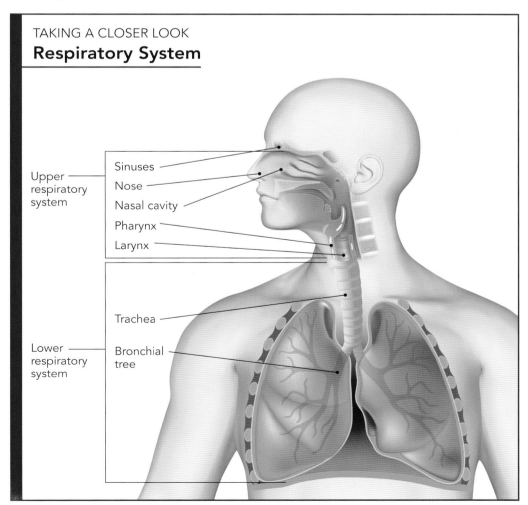

TAKING A CLOSER LOOK
Respiratory System

Upper respiratory system
- Sinuses
- Nose
- Nasal cavity
- Pharynx
- Larynx

Lower respiratory system
- Trachea
- Bronchial tree

the branching tubes of the bronchial tree, and the lungs. The *trachea* — pronounced "trā'-kē-uh" — is the windpipe. The trachea and the bronchial ("bron'-kē-ul") tree conduct air to and from your lungs and distribute that air through them. The tubes that branch off of the trachea (the *bronchi*) keep on branching into smaller and smaller tubes (*bronchioles* and finally *terminal bronchioles*), just like a tree.

"Upper" and "lower" of course only refer to the general location of the parts of the respiratory system. A doctor might say that a patient has an "upper respiratory infection" to refer to something like a head cold or sinus infection or a "lower respiratory infection" when referring to bronchitis or pneumonia. We'll learn more about these problems later.

Another way to think about the parts of the respiratory system is by describing the sort of function the parts have. Some parts of the respiratory carry air from place to place. Other parts of the respiratory system are designed to get oxygen from the air into the blood and to get carbon dioxide out of the blood and into the air to be exhaled. This is called "gas exchange," because oxygen and carbon dioxide enter and leave the body as gases. During gas exchange in the lungs, oxygen and carbon dioxide sort of trade places.

Many parts of the respiratory system conduct air from outside the body to the areas in the lungs where gas exchange takes place. Inhaled air moves through the nose, nasal cavity, pharynx, larynx, trachea, bronchi, bronchioles, and terminal bronchioles, in that order. The nose and other parts of the upper respiratory system filter, warm, and humidify inspired air long before it reaches the lungs.

After air is conducted to the farthest reaches of the lungs, gas exchange finally takes place. Air enters alveoli, tiny thin-walled sacs, where it is able to be close enough to the blood in capillaries for oxygen and carbon dioxide to move between the blood and air. Oxygen from inspired air is taken into the blood. Carbon dioxide from the blood is released into the alveoli to be removed with the expired air.

The Nose

The nose is probably the most overlooked part of the respiratory system. After all, it just sticks out from our face, right? I mean, it doesn't do anything, right? Well, it does hold people's glasses, but other than that…

In reality, the nose is very important, and does much more than provide a place for eyeglasses to rest. Let's take a closer look.

The nose is the beginning of the respiratory system. The two openings on the nose are called the *external nares*, or nostrils. Air, of course, can bypass the nostrils when you breathe through your mouth, but that air misses out on some of the important things the nostrils, nasal passages, and sinuses do. The nose is far more than just an opening for air. The nostrils, or nares, provide the ideal entrance to the respiratory system.

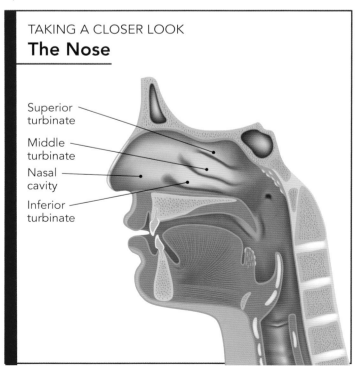

TAKING A CLOSER LOOK
The Nose

Superior turbinate

Middle turbinate

Nasal cavity

Inferior turbinate

When the air passes through the nares, it enters the nasal cavity. In the nose are coarse hairs that help filter out dust particles. This cleaning action minimizes the amount of foreign material that finds its way to the lungs.

Inspired air then passes over the lining of the nasal cavity. This lining is not ordinary skin but instead is a "mucous membrane." Mucous membrane is thin and far more moist and supple than skin, and it is rich in small veins and capillaries. Warm blood flowing through these blood vessels helps warm cold air as it passes over the mucous membrane. The moisture produced by the mucous membrane humidifies the air. The gooey mucus, coating the mucous membranes, traps lots of dust and bacteria. Tiny hairs on the mucous membrane, called *cilia*, sweep this mucus and the debris stuck in it toward the

Sneezing

A sneeze is a very forceful expulsion of air from the nose and mouth. Everyone sneezes at one time or another.

Why do we sneeze?

As it turns out, there is a pretty simple explanation.

Anything that irritates the nasal lining can trigger a sneeze. This might be an irritation

due to dust particles or pollen. It could be irritation from a cold virus. Exposure to fumes, say a perfume or a strong household cleaner, can cause enough irritation to trigger a sneeze.

When nerve fibers in the nasal lining detect the irritation, a nerve reflex is triggered. This reflex causes muscles in the chest and throat to contract vigorously. The result is a powerful release of air from the mouth and nose; that is, a sneeze! The purpose of the sneeze is to expel the mucus that contains the things that are irritating the membranes.

A sneeze can fire air out of your body at over 100 miles per hour. Air traveling at that speed can make a really loud sound! One sneeze can shoot out 40,000 droplets containing thousands of germs — and the mucus-containing droplets propelled by a sneeze can travel quite a distance, sometimes ending up on someone else's mucous membranes. Yuck. Simply covering your nose and mouth when you sneeze helps stop germs from spreading.

There are some common misconceptions about sneezing. First of all, the heart does not stop when you sneeze. Doesn't happen. Next, your eyes cannot pop out of your head when you sneeze. Although the natural tendency is for the eyelids to be closed during a sneeze, if the eyelids are held open, the eyeballs won't pop out. Promise.

Mucosa

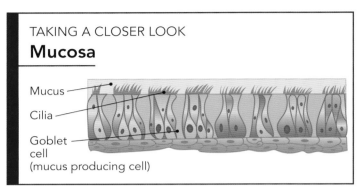

Mucus

Cilia

Goblet cell (mucus producing cell)

throat where it can be swallowed and destroyed in the stomach. Already you can see that the nose and nasal cavity are a built-in air purifier and conditioner protecting your lower airways and lungs.

The mucous membranes in the nasal cavity are designed to secrete lots of mucus. By the way, notice the spelling here. *Mucous* membranes make *mucus*.[1] Mucus is a gel-like coating produced by the mucous membrane lining our nose, sinuses, mouth, throat, lungs, digestive tract, and even our eyelids.

Mucus might sound yucky, but it is very important. The mucus that is made in the nasal cavity not only moistens the air but helps trap pollen, dust particles, and bacteria. It is a very important part of the defense system in our respiratory tract. Mucus contains special enzymes, like lysozyme, that help destroy bacteria. Mucus even contains molecules that attract helpful bacteria-eating viruses! (These are called bacteriophages.) God designed mucous membranes and the mucus they produce to clean up and condition air before it enters our bodies.

God's design for cleaning up our inspired air goes beyond this wonderful goo coating the inside of our nose. Our nose and nasal cavity does not provide a straight path for the air passing through. Instead, they contain shelves and barriers that force the air to flow over the surface of a lot of mucous membrane. There are, for instance, three shelf-like *nasal conchae* (pronounced "kong'-kē") sticking out from each side of the nasal cavity. (These are also called *turbinates*.) They disrupt the straight flow of air and thus stir it up. By maximizing air's contact with the mucous membranes in the nasal passages, each breath of inspired air has plenty of opportunity to get warmed or cooled to within a degree of your body's temperature and moistened. The circuitous route air takes protects the upper airway and lungs from harsh, cold, dry air when you are outside on a cold day.

Sinuses

Have you ever heard somebody say, "If you believe that, you've got a hole in your head"? Actually, you do have holes in your head. In fact, we all do. And it's no joke. We need those holes in our heads!

Sinuses

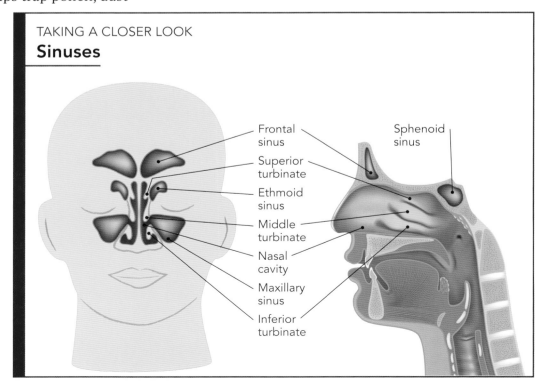

Frontal sinus

Superior turbinate

Ethmoid sinus

Middle turbinate

Nasal cavity

Maxillary sinus

Inferior turbinate

Sphenoid sinus

---

1 Mucous is an adjective, but mucus is a noun.

Surrounding the nasal cavity are several air-filled spaces in the skull. Connected to the nasal cavity by small passageways, these air-filled spaces are called *sinuses*. There are four sinuses, and they exist in pairs, one on each side of the nasal cavity. They are the frontal, maxillary, ethmoid, and sphenoid sinuses. You can see these in the illustration. These sinuses are located in hollowed-out spaces in the skull, but they are lined with mucous membrane just like the nasal cavity itself. The frontal sinuses are in your forehead. The maxillary sinuses are below your eyes. The ethmoid and sphenoid sinuses are located deeper behind your face.

The membranes that line the sinuses are continuous with those in the nasal cavities. Mucus that is produced in the sinuses ultimately drains through the passageways connecting them to the nasal cavity and into the nasal cavity itself. Once there, it can be blown out if you blow your nose or drain down your throat to your stomach, where stomach acid can kill any germs that might be left alive.

The sinuses have several functions. First of all, they help decrease the weight of the skull. If the sinus cavities were solid bone, the facial part of the skull would be much heavier. Secondly, as in the nasal cavity, the sinuses defend your body from germs, dirt, and cold, dry, irritating air. The mucus in the sinuses helps trap and kill bacteria. The sinuses warm and humidify the air that passes through them. Finally, the sinuses add some resonance to the voice by adding chambers for vibrating air to bounce around. Consider how different a friend's voice sounds when he or she has a bad cold.

Not bad for a few holes in your head!

The Pharynx

The next part of the respiratory system is the pharynx. The pharynx is commonly called the throat. It is a funnel-shaped tube that begins at the rear of the nasal cavity and extends down to the larynx (voice box). In order, air passes through three regions of the pharynx: the nasopharynx, the oropharynx, and the laryngopharynx. As you might guess, the prefix on each of these big words simply refers to the nearest landmark — the nose (*naso*), the mouth (*oro*), and the larynx (*laryngo*).

The nasopharynx is the superior (upper) portion of the pharynx. It begins at the rear of the nasal cavity and extends as far as the soft palate. The *soft palate* is the rear portion of the roof of the mouth. When you swallow, the soft palate moves enough to close off the nasal cavity from the nasopharynx. This prevents food from getting into the nasal cavity. If you've ever managed to inadvertently get some of your soda past your soft palate and up into the back of your nose while coughing or laughing, you know that you should thank our Lord for giving you a soft palate to make that a very rare occurrence!

The nasal cavity and the soft palate mark the upper and lower boundaries of the nasopharynx, but there is another way for air and small amounts of fluid to enter and leave it. The nasopharynx communicates

TAKING A CLOSER LOOK
The Pharnyx

Eustachian tube opening

Nasopharynx

Oropharynx

Laryngopharynx

Larynx

with each middle ear via a tiny tube. These *phar-yngotympanic tubes* are also known as *Eustachian tubes*, named after the 16th-century anatomist who discovered them, Bartolomeo Eustachi. These small tubes drain any excess mucus or other fluid that might collect in the middle ear and empty it into this portion the pharynx. The Eustachian tubes also help equalize the pressure between the atmosphere around you and the middle ear.

If you have ever been in an airplane or on a tall mountain and felt your ears "pop," you understand the value of the Eustachian tubes. You might have had to yawn to encourage the tiny Eustachian tubes to open enough to equalize the air pressure outside your body (and therefore inside your mouth and throat) with the air pressure inside your middle ear. Didn't your hearing suddenly improve once your ears "popped"? You see, the middle ear is the part of your ear where the vibrating eardrum (*tympanic membrane*) transfers sound vibrations to three tiny bones, making it possible for you to ear. If the air pressure inside your middle ear is different from the air pressure outside of your body, the eardrum cannot vibrate freely and your hearing is temporarily impaired. By equalizing the air pressure between your throat — the *pharynx* — and the eardrum — the *tympanic membrane* — the *pharyngotympanic tubes* (see how they got that big name?) restore your hearing to normal.

The *oropharynx* is the middle part of the pharynx. It is the part of the throat that is behind your mouth, or *oral cavity*. The oropharynx extends from the soft palate down to the level of the hyoid bone, which is located just below the level of the chin. The *hyoid bone* is a small U-shaped bone that supports your tongue. The hyoid bone does not have any joints with

Ear Infection

Have you ever had an ear infection? Middle ear infections are called *otitis* (meaning "ear inflammation") *media* (meaning "middle"). Acute otitis media causes a great deal of pain, sometimes with fever. Though anyone can develop an ear infection, it is more common in babies and young children. Acute otitis media is associated with fluid accumulation in the middle ear as well as bulging and redness of the eardrum.

Acute otitis media is usually caused by bacteria. How, you might well wonder, do bacteria manage to get into the middle ear? Typically, they move up through malfunctioning Eustachian tubes. When a sore throat, allergy symptoms, or exposure to tobacco smoke causes inflammation of the nasopharynx, the Eustachian tubes may swell and fail to drain properly. Eventually, because the air pressure in the middle ear cannot easily equalize with atmospheric pressure, negative pressure develops in the middle ear. This negative pressure can then pull bacteria-containing fluid — even the milk a baby sucks from its bottle — up the Eustachian tube and into the middle ear.

Ear infections are more common in the young because their Eustachian tubes are shorter, smaller in diameter, and more horizontal than those of adults. Therefore, their Eustachian tubes swell shut more easily and, being shorter, bacteria-laden fluid only has to make a short trip to reach the middle ear.

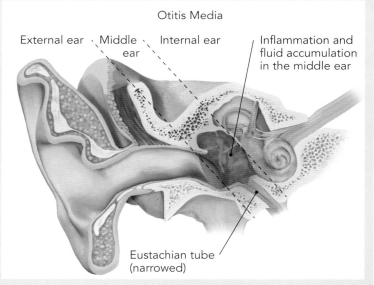

Otitis Media

External ear · Middle · Internal ear | Inflammation and fluid accumulation in the middle ear
ear

Eustachian tube (narrowed)

other bones but is held in place by ligaments and muscles that help move your tongue and voice box.

The nasopharynx and the oropharynx are not just tubes through which air passes. They are also the home of your tonsils. The *adenoid tonsils* are located in the back of your nasopharynx. The *palatine tonsils* and the *lingual tonsils* are located in the oropharynx. The lingual tonsils are located at the back of your tongue. The palatine tonsils look like two pink mounds on each side of the oropharynx. Because they are exposed to germs entering your body, the tonsils are an important part of your immune system. Like policemen guarding this gateway to your respiratory system, the

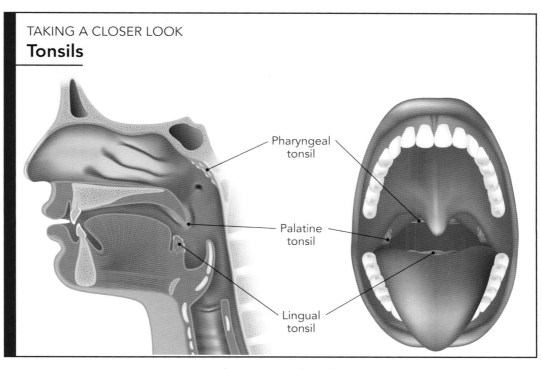

TAKING A CLOSER LOOK
Tonsils

Pharyngeal tonsil

Palatine tonsil

Lingual tonsil

tonsils contain white blood cells that help your body recognize and fight infection. Sometimes tonsils are surgically removed with a *tonsillectomy* if they become persistently swollen or severely infected.

Snoring

Snoring is very common. Snoring is caused by a partial obstruction of airflow through the mouth, nose, or throat. Vibration of the obstructing structures or the squeezing of air through a narrowed passage produces the low-pitched noise that may disturb the snoring person's sleep or keep others awake.

Swelling in the nasal passages due to allergies, enlarged tonsils and adenoids, a deviated septum (a crookedness in the wall separating the nostrils), an unusually long uvula, and excessive relaxation of the tongue or throat muscles are just some of the causes of snoring. Men are more likely to snore than women, and overweight people with a lot of bulky tissue in the neck are also more likely to snore.

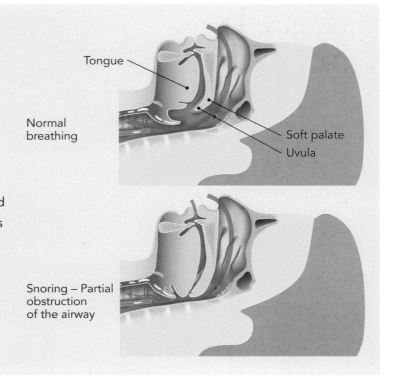

Tongue

Normal breathing

Soft palate

Uvula

Snoring – Partial obstruction of the airway

The third part of the pharynx, the laryngopharynx, begins at the level of the hyoid bone and ends at the larynx. Upon leaving the laryngopharynx, inspired air is permitted by an anatomical gate called the epiglottis to continue on its path to your lungs. The epiglottis slams shut, however, if food or liquids are passing by, and directs them toward your esophagus and on to the stomach. We'll see in the next section how the epiglottis is designed.

The Larynx

The larynx is the portion of the airway that connects the laryngopharynx to the trachea. It is often called the "voice box." The larynx protects the trachea from foreign material entering from above and transforms exhaled air into speech and song.

Several pieces of cartilage form the larynx. The three largest are called the thyroid cartilage, the cricoid cartilage, and the epiglottis. The epiglottis is like a trap door at the top of the larynx, and below it is the most prominent cartilage, the *thyroid cartilage*. The thyroid cartilage, commonly called the "Adam's apple," is visible on the front of your neck and moves up and down as you swallow. You can feel a little notch on the top of the thyroid cartilage with your finger. It is called the "thyroid" cartilage because the thyroid gland is draped over part of it. Below the thyroid cartilage is the *cricoid cartilage*. The cricoid cartilage is shaped like a signet ring, and it completely encircles the top of the trachea, to which it is attached. The broader part of this signet ring forms the lower rear wall of the larynx and the thin part of the cricoid ring is located in front.

Supported within these larger cartilages forming the outer walls of the larynx are smaller ones that support the vocal folds, tissues that vibrate to produce sounds as air passes over them. These are called the arytenoid, cuneiform, and corniculate cartilages.

The epiglottis guards the entrance to the larynx from above, protecting it from the things you eat and drink. The epiglottis is a leaf-shaped flap of elastic cartilage. The "stem" portion is anchored to the anterior rim of the thyroid cartilage and acts like a hinge for this doorway to the airways. The broader (or "leaf") end of the epiglottis is unattached, allowing the epiglottis to swing up and down like a trap door. When we swallow, the larynx moves upward and, at the same time, the epiglottis flaps down to close off the airways below. This movement of the epiglottis helps direct food and drink into the esophagus and keeps them out of our lungs.

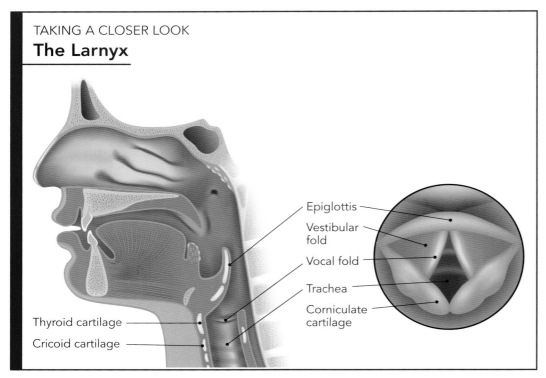

TAKING A CLOSER LOOK
The Larnyx

Epiglottis
Vestibular fold
Vocal fold
Trachea
Corniculate cartilage
Thyroid cartilage
Cricoid cartilage

Just below the attachment point of the epiglottis, the mucosa (mucous membrane) lining the airway forms two sets of folds. The superior and thicker ones are the *vestibular folds*, or "false vocal cords." As you might guess from this name, this pair of folds does not participate in sound production, but they do help close off the glottis while you speak.

Inferior to the vestibular folds are the *vocal folds*, or "true vocal cords." Muscles in the larynx can tighten or relax the vocal folds as needed to produce higher and lower sounds as air passes over them and to move the cartilages supporting them to begin

"shaping" the sounds into words. The area of the larynx that contains the vocal cords is known as the *glottis*. (The epiglottis is located *above* the glottis: the prefix *epi* means "above.")

Let's look more closely at the way God designed human anatomy to allow you to speak and sing.

The Voice

Some people don't talk much. Some people talk way too much. Most of us are somewhere in between.

Our Creator has given us a great gift. This is the gift of speech. The ability to speak allows us to communicate and interact with one another in ways that other creatures cannot.

So how does it work?

When we speak or sing, we force air from our lungs through the glottis and past the true vocal cords. As the air passes the vocal cords, the vocal cords vibrate. Muscles in the larynx can increase or decrease the tension on the vocal cords, causing a change in the sound. When vocal cords are more relaxed, they vibrate slower, resulting in a lower pitch. Alternatively, when vocal cords are tighter, they vibrate most rapidly, resulting in a higher pitch.

As a general rule, men have lower voices than women. This is because due to the effect of androgens (male sex hormones) men have slightly longer and thicker vocal cords.

But it is not just the vocal cords alone that produce speech. The nasal and oral cavities, as well as the sinuses, contribute to the resonance of our voices. The movement of the tongue, lips, and pharynx help mold sound into recognizable speech. The force with which air is pushed from the lungs past the vocal cords plays a very important role in the loudness of our voice.

Laryngitis

Laryngitis is an inflammation of the larynx. It can result in hoarseness or even a complete, though temporary, loss of voice.

Inflammation of the vocal cords (vocal folds) can cause swelling and pain, keeping them from moving normally during speech. In severe cases, the swelling can be so extensive as to almost prevent the vocal cords from vibrating.

Laryngitis can be caused by viral or bacterial infections, allergies, or inhalation of chemical fumes. Irritation of the larynx can also result from chemical burns caused by stomach acid that sometimes percolates up the esophagus and slips over into the larynx. This is called *acid reflux disease*. Overuse of the voice can lead to inflammation of the vocal cords. Irritation caused by cigarettes or alcohol can also cause laryngitis.

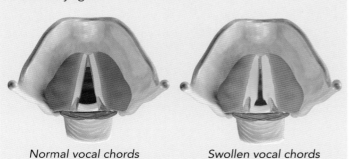

Normal vocal chords   *Swollen vocal chords*

The Trachea

The *trachea*, or windpipe, begins at the larynx and runs down into the chest. It is a tube about 5 inches long and 1 inch in diameter. The trachea branches into the two main *bronchi*, one *bronchus* for each lung.

The wall of the trachea has four layers: mucosa, submucosa, hyaline cartilage, and adventitia.

Like the other airways in the respiratory system, the trachea is much more than a tube. The trachea, as well as most of the airways we are discussing, is lined with a mucous membrane that produces dust-catching mucus and sweeps it away with microscopic cilia. The inner layers of the trachea — the mucosa and and submucosa beneath it — are packed with mucus-producing *goblet cells*. The mucosa is also loaded with *ciliated cells*. Cilia — hairlike projections from the ciliated cells — continually move mucus containing dust and debris toward the pharynx.

TAKING A CLOSER LOOK
The Trachea

Larynx

Tracheal cartilages

Location of carina (internal ridge)

Trachea

Root of the left lung

Root of the right lung

Lung tissue

Primary bronchi

Secondary bronchi

Heimlich Maneuver

Occasionally a person may have his or her airway completely blocked by a piece of food. This is obviously a medical emergency. The obstruction must be removed immediately.

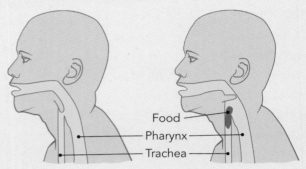

Food
Pharynx
Trachea

In recent years, a procedure known as the Heimlich maneuver was developed to enable laymen with some knowledge of first aid to help in these emergencies, sometimes providing life-saving help long before medical professionals could arrive. This maneuver involves exerting sudden pressure on the victim's upper abdomen just below the diaphragm. This sudden compression would ideally push air into the trachea with enough force to dislodge the obstruction and open the airway. However, it is easy to injure someone with this maneuver (such as fracturing a rib or the end of the sternum), so care must be taken when attempting to perform this on a person. The point at which pressure should be applied in the Heimlich maneuver varies in children and adults.

Some medical experts favor back slaps or chest thrusts (or a combination of both) to aid choking victims.

Emergency Tracheotomy

While the Heimlich maneuver is a procedure that anyone can learn to perform safely, an emergency *tracheotomy* — despite what you might have seen on television — is far riskier. (*Trache* means "trachea" and *otomy* means "opening.") If a choking person is completely unable to move any air at all past an obstructed trachea, and despite repeated attempts to clear the obstruction with the Heimlich maneuver and abdominal thrusts, is still unable to even gasp or cough, it may become necessary to open the trachea surgically to allow life-saving air to enter the lungs.

Actual emergency tracheotomies are extremely difficult to perform without proper medical training and equipment. Therefore, in a life-threatening situation outside a hospital, the procedure normally used as a last resort is not a tracheotomy but a *cricothyrotomy* (though many people still call this a tracheotomy). An actual tracheotomy is placed between tracheal rings, but a *cricothyrotomy* is a surgical opening placed higher on the trachea, between the cricoid cartilage and the thyroid cartilage (Adam's apple). This opening is below the place ordinarily plugged by a misdirected bit of food or other foreign body, and once a small tube is placed in the surgical opening in the cricothyroid membrane, air can enter the lungs.

Despite the apparent ease of this procedure in television drama, even a cricothyrotomy in the hands of an untrained person is extremely risky. A thorough knowledge of anatomy and the techniques involved in the procedure are needed to safely navigate the many major blood vessels and nerves in the neck.

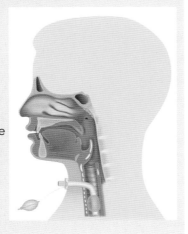

While the cilia in the nasal cavity direct mucus down toward the pharynx, cilia in the trachea sweep mucus upward away from the lungs and toward the pharynx. In this manner, the lining of the trachea works like the lining of the nasal cavity in protecting and cleaning the airway. God has designed every part of our bodies with the details it takes to protect us.

Below its mucosa and submucosa, the trachea is supported by 16 to 20 rings of hyaline cartilage. Without these sturdy "C" shaped rings of vertically stacked cartilage, the trachea could collapse and air movement would stop. Dense connective tissue holds the cartilage rings together. The openings of each "C" face posteriorly (to the back) toward the esophagus. (The esophagus is the tube connecting the throat to the stomach, and it is right behind the trachea.) These rings of cartilage keep the airway open despite the pressure changes that occur in the trachea during inspiration and expiration.

The outer layer of the trachea is adventita. This layer is composed of connective tissue that helps secure the trachea to surrounding structures.

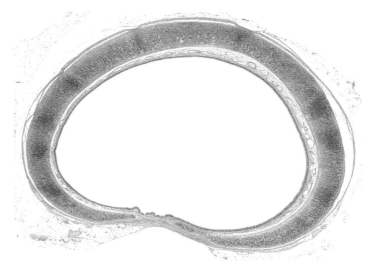

Cross section of the trachea, showing C-shaped tracheal rings of hyaline cartilage. Ciliated mucosa lines the trachea.

Bronchi and Bronchioles

The trachea ends by dividing into two *bronchi*. The *right primary bronchus* goes to the right lung, and the *left primary bronchus* goes to the left lung. As the bronchi continue into the lungs, they branch more and more, much in the same way that blood vessels branch the farther they are from the main blood vessels. These airways are at times called the "bronchial tree."

The primary (first) bronchi divide to become the *secondary bronchi*. There is one secondary bronchus for each lobe of the lung, so secondary bronchi are also called the *lobar bronchi*. Since the right lung has three lobes, and the left lung has two lobes, there are three lobar bronchi on the right and two lobar bronchi on the left.

The secondary bronchi divide to form the *tertiary bronchi* which supply air to segments of the lung (and are therefore also called *segmental bronchi*). Tertiary bronchi then divide to form bronchioles. Bronchioles are much smaller in diameter than bronchi and do not have any cartilage in their walls to keep them open. Instead, they are held open by elastic fibers that attach them to the surrounding lung tissue. The bronchioles continue to divide, getting smaller and smaller, until they become *terminal bronchioles*. The terminal bronchioles are the end of the air-conducting part of the respiratory system.[2]

The structures past the terminal bronchioles are involved in gas exchange. Terminal bronchioles branch to form *respiratory bron-*

chioles, tiny airways studded with gas-exchanging *alveoli*. Respiratory bronchioles divide into *alveolar ducts*, which are also studded with outpocketing alveoli. Each alveolar duct ends in an open space into which grape-like clusters of alveoli open. A person develops new alveoli until he or she is about eight years old, by which time the average person has about 300 million of them. Do you get the idea that alveoli are important?

The Lungs

The lungs are the organs in the body responsible for both ventilation and respiration. Respiration is the process in the lungs that gets oxygen into the blood and carbon dioxide out of the blood. Here we are referring specifically to external respiration, which is gas exchange in the lungs. *Internal respiration* is gas exchange between capillaries and the cells and tissues of the body. *Cellular respiration* is the process by which cells obtain energy from nutrients like glucose.

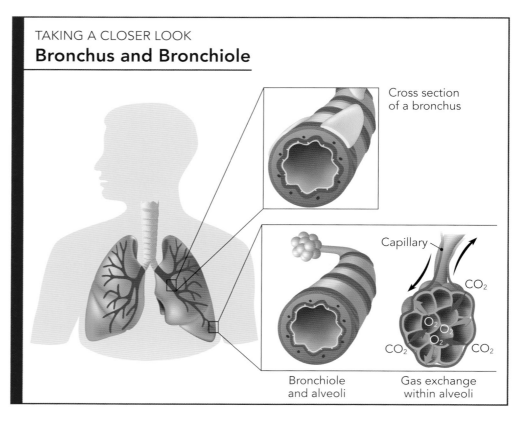

TAKING A CLOSER LOOK
Bronchus and Bronchiole

Cross section of a bronchus

Capillary

CO_2

O_2

O_2 O_2

CO_2

CO_2

Bronchiole and alveoli

Gas exchange within alveoli

Asthma

Do you have a family member or a friend who has asthma? There is a good chance that you do. Though it varies in severity, about 8 percent of the population in the United States suffers from asthma. That works out to about 1 person in 12, and that's significant.

Asthma is a chronic inflammatory disease of the airways. It is characterized by intermittent spasm of the airways. That means that

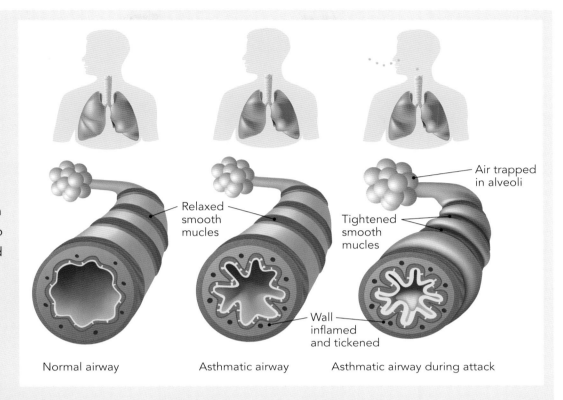

Normal airway   Asthmatic airway   Asthmatic airway during attack

Labels: Relaxed smooth mucles; Tightened smooth mucles; Air trapped in alveoli; Wall inflamed and tickened

parts of the airways constrict for varying periods of time, making it difficult to exhale or inhale. As you can imagine, this is very uncomfortable and frightening, and it can sometimes become dangerous. Symptoms typically include shortness of breath, cough, and wheezing. Wheezing is the noise produced when air squeezes through a tight space. Wheezing can occur during expiration and during inspiration. The symptoms are often intermittent. In other words, patients can be without symptoms one minute and then suddenly develop severe shortness of breath.

Our understanding of the cause of asthma has improved greatly in recent years. In the past it was thought that asthma was caused primarily by the contraction of the smooth muscle in the airways. This contraction narrowed the airways and made movement of the air into and out of the lungs very difficult. More recently, the role of inflammation in asthma has been much better recognized. This improved understanding of the cause of asthma has led to better treatment for the disease. In the past, the goal was to relieve the airway constriction. Today, the primary goal is to relieve, or at least minimize, the inflammation in the airways.

Asthma can be triggered by many things. Infections, either viral or bacterial, are an obvious trigger. Exposure to cold air, exercise, allergies, and exposure to irritants, such as perfumes, household chemicals, or cigarette smoke can also exacerbate asthma.

Treatment of asthma is focused primarily on minimizing the inflammation in the airways. Long-term management usually includes the use of inhaled corticosteroids (to minimize the chronic inflammation), and often includes long-acting medications called bronchodilators (medication aims at relieving the construction of the airways). These medications are often administered by small hand-held inhalers. Sudden attacks of asthma are often treated with fast-acting bronchodilators designed to help quickly relieve airway obstruction.

Air must reach the lungs in order for respiration to happen. *Ventilation* gets air into the lungs. Ventilation just means "breathing." It is the process of moving air from the environment into the lungs (inspiration, or inhalation) and then moving air back out (expiration, or exhalation). Without lungs, air would not be drawn in through our airways, and with no way to get oxygen into our blood we would die in minutes.

Gross Anatomy

The human body has two lungs, one on each side of the chest cavity. The lungs are separated from each other by the heart and large blood vessels in the *mediastinum*. Each lung is somewhat cone shaped, broader at the bottom and rounded at the top. The inferior portion of the lung is called the base. The base of the lung sits on the diaphragm. The superior portion of the lung is called the apex.

On the medial surface of each lung is the hilum. The *hilum* is where the bronchi and blood vessels enter the lungs.

The right and left lungs are not identical. The right lung is slightly larger than the left. The right lung has three lobes, and the left lung has only two. Can you think of why? There has to be room for the heart! The left lung has a concave depression that accommodates the heart.

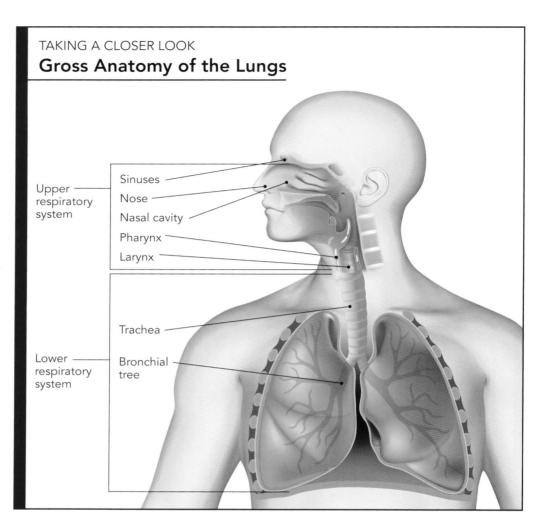

TAKING A CLOSER LOOK
Gross Anatomy of the Lungs

Upper respiratory system
- Sinuses
- Nose
- Nasal cavity
- Pharynx
- Larynx

Lower respiratory system
- Trachea
- Bronchial tree

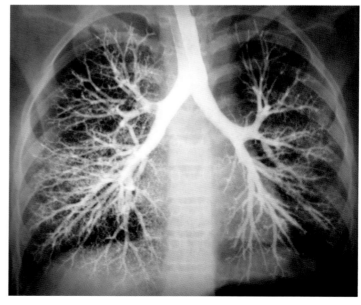

X-ray demonstrating the extensive branching of the bronchial tree.

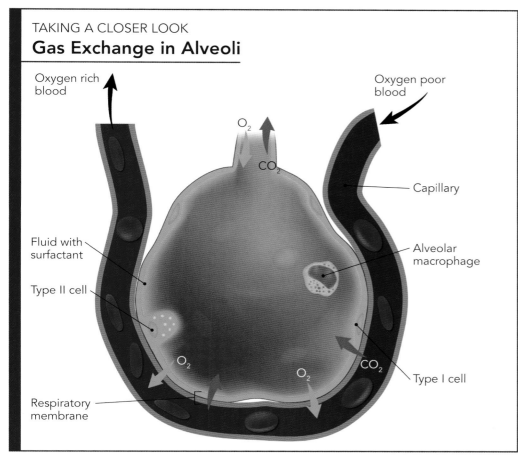

TAKING A CLOSER LOOK
Gas Exchange in Alveoli

Oxygen rich blood

Oxygen poor blood

O_2

CO_2

Capillary

Fluid with surfactant

Alveolar macrophage

Type II cell

O_2

O_2

CO_2

Type I cell

Respiratory membrane

An alveolus can, in some ways, be compared to a balloon or a bubble. It is a small cavity that is made of a single layer of squamous epithelium. These epithelial cells are known as type I alveolar cells. Type I cells are responsible for the structure of the alveolar wall, making up 95 to 97 percent of the alveolar lining. These cells are extremely thin. This allows the most efficient gas exchange possible.

The outer surface of the alveolus is covered by a mesh of capillaries. At this point, the air in the respiratory system and the blood in the circulatory system are brought very close together. As you recall, capillary walls are also very thin. A thin capillary wall

Alveoli

Gas exchange happens across the walls of little sacs called *alveoli*. Alveoli are like tiny sacs that pooch out from the walls of respiratory bronchioles and alveolar ducts, the smallest airways in the bronchial tree. Some estimates suggest that there are as many as 2 million alveolar ducts in each lung! The alveolar ducts end in clusters of *alveoli* called *alveolar sacs*. Alveolar sacs look like microscopic clusters of grapes.

One *alveolus* (the plural form of alveolus is *alveoli*) is a microscopic air sac. It is the endpoint of the respiratory system. Alveoli are the "grapes" that make up alveolar sacs. Gases are exchanged between the air in the respiratory tree and the blood in capillaries draped on the alveoli. Oxygen and carbon dioxide move across their thin walls and the thin walls of the capillaries.

adjacent to a thin alveolar wall is the best possible design for the efficient movement of gases in and out of the bloodstream. Remember, you have at least 300 million alveoli in each of your lungs. That's a lot of alveoli, giving you a HUGE surface area for gas exchange!

Is this another example of the incredible design of the human body, or did this happen by chance? Does this cause us to stop and give praise to our wonderful Creator, or do we merely accept that this is the result of chemicals randomly banging together over millions of years? That's not really a hard choice, is it?

In addition to the type I cells in the alveolus, there is another important cell found there. Incredibly enough, these are called type II alveolar cells (clever, huh?). The type II cells secrete alveolar fluid. This fluid keeps the surface of the alveolus moist. The most important component of this alveolar fluid is surfactant. *Surfactant* is a special kind of molecule that has some detergent-like properties. It aids in reducing the surface tension of the alveolar fluid, and that helps prevent the alveolus from collapsing. Surfactant helps alveoli stay open like the soap bubbles children blow through the air for fun.

There are also macrophages in the alveolus. These cells can move along the surface of the alveolus. Macrophages are like cellular vacuum cleaners. They keep the alveolus free from dust and debris.

Blood Vessels

Blood enters the lungs by two different arterial pathways. One of these brings blood to the lungs to pick up oxygen for the body to use. The other brings blood for the lungs themselves to use.

The first pathway by which blood reaches the lungs we have already studied, namely, the pulmonary arteries. As you remember, deoxygenated blood enters the lungs via the right and left *pulmonary arteries*. These arteries enter the hilum of each lung and then branch to get smaller and smaller until they become the capillaries that surround the alveoli.

Pneumonia

Pneumonia is an inflammatory condition of the lungs. It primarily affects the air sacs, the alveoli. The most common cause of this inflammation is infection, either bacterial or viral. Other causes include autoimmune disease or exposure to certain drugs. A particularly dangerous type of pneumonia occurs when stomach contents are aspirated into the lungs (so-called aspiration pneumonia), causing acid damage to the lining of the airways.

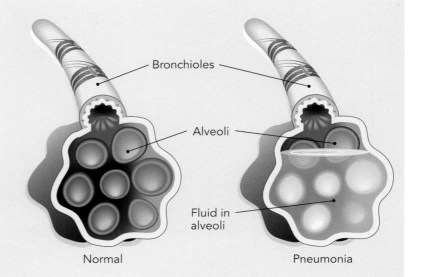

Pneumonia is characterized by cough, fever, and shortness of breath. Chest x-rays are very helpful in diagnosing pneumonia. The inflamed areas of the lung are often seen clearly on the x-ray film. If the cause of the pneumonia is bacterial, it can be helpful to obtain samples of the patient's sputum for testing. This can help determine the type of bacteria causing the infection.

The severity of pneumonia ranges from relatively mild to life threatening. The most common treatment for pneumonia is antibiotics. Management of pneumonia can also at times include supplemental oxygen, breathing treatments, and intravenous fluids. In the most severe cases, patients can be placed on a ventilator (a machine designed to move air in and out of the lungs).

Pneumonia is the eighth leading cause of death in the United States. It is most common in very young children (under age 5) and in adults over age 75.

Risk factors for pneumonia (other than age) include a history of smoking, alcoholism, liver or kidney disease, and illnesses that suppress or weaken the immune system, such as cancer.

After the blood is oxygenated, it exits the lungs via the pulmonary veins on its way back to the heart. The heart, of course, sends this oxygenated blood out to the brain and the rest of the body.

So why, you might wonder, would the lungs need an additional way to receive blood? You probably remember that the heart is full of blood but still has to have a special set of coronary arteries to supply the heart muscle itself with oxygen and nutrients. The same is true of the lungs. Though they are filled with air containing up to 21 percent oxygen as well as miles of capillaries devoted to capturing some of this oxygen for the body to use, the lungs need their own dedicated supply of oxygenated blood.

That other important arterial pathway bringing blood to the lungs involves the *bronchial arteries*. Like the coronary arteries that supply the heart muscle, bronchial arteries arise from the aorta and, like the pulmonary arteries, enter each lung at the hilum. Bronchial arteries supply *oxygenated* blood and nutrients to the lung tissue. Most of the blood from the bronchial arteries returns to the heart through the pulmonary veins, and some returns via the bronchial veins that empty into the superior vena cava.

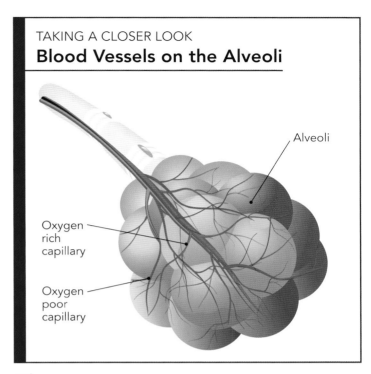

TAKING A CLOSER LOOK
Blood Vessels on the Alveoli

Alveoli

Oxygen rich capillary

Oxygen poor capillary

Pleura

Each lung is enclosed by its own double-layered membrane called the *pleura*. The layer of the pleura that covers the surface of the lung is called the *visceral pleura*. The pleural layer adjacent to the interior of the chest wall is called the *parietal pleura*.

Surfactant

You may have heard of premature babies that have difficulty breathing when they are born. While a baby is inside the mother's womb, the baby does not have to use lungs to exchange gases. Gas exchange takes place between the baby's blood and the mother's blood through the placenta. But as soon as a baby is born, he or she must take a breath to expand the alveoli in the lungs. From then on, it is the job of the baby's lungs to obtain oxygen and remove carbon dioxide from the blood. If there were no surfactant in the alveoli, the baby would have difficulty breathing because many of the alveoli would soon collapse.

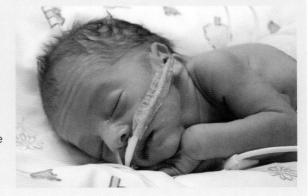

God has designed a baby's lungs to begin making surfactant just a few weeks before the time to be born. If the baby is born too soon, he or she may have difficulty breathing because the surfactant is not yet present. Intensive care facilities today can assist a premature baby to breathe and even provide artificial surfactant until the baby's lungs can catch up with production.

Recall the example we used when illustrating the pericardium. If you take a balloon partially filled with air and slowly press your fist into it, you get the idea. Your fist will be inside a two-layered membrane. This illustration helps describe the pericardium as well as the pleura.

Cells in the pleura produce a small amount of liquid that helps lubricate the potential space between the visceral and parietal pleural surfaces. This is called *pleural fluid*. It reduces friction between the pleural layers and allows the lungs to expand and contract more easily. Even though the pleural layers glide across each other easily, the surface tension produced by the pleural fluid makes it very difficult to actually separate the layers. This helps keep the lungs expanded inside the chest cavity.

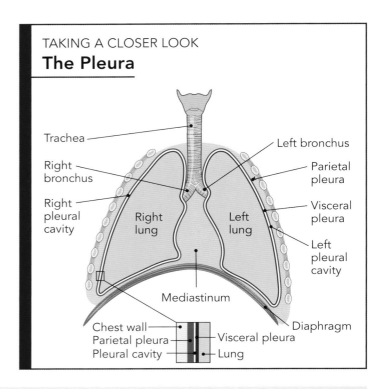

TAKING A CLOSER LOOK
The Pleura

Trachea

Left bronchus

Right bronchus

Parietal pleura

Right pleural cavity

Right lung

Left lung

Visceral pleura

Left pleural cavity

Mediastinum

Chest wall

Parietal pleura

Pleural cavity

Visceral pleura

Lung

Diaphragm

Pleural Problems

As we described, the visceral layer of the pleura covers the surface of the lung, and the parietal layer of the pleura covers the inner surface of the chest wall. These layers glide across one another, but due to surface tension they rarely separate. However, on occasion the pleural space can be compromised due to illness or injury.

One of the more common problems occurs when the pleural membranes become inflamed. This is known as *pleurisy*. Pleurisy can result in severe pain when taking a breath. The pain results from the inflamed membranes rubbing against each other. (Think of how uncomfortable it is when something rubs against your skin when you have sunburn, and you'll get the idea.) Pleurisy is often the result of an infection, for example, pneumonia. However, other diseases can cause it.

At times, fluid can leak into the pleural cavity. When blood collects in the pleural cavity, it is called a hemothorax. This can be the result of a traumatic injury to the lung.

In other situations, watery (serous) fluid accumulates in the pleural cavity. This is called a *pleural effusion*. Effusions can have many causes such as infection, malignancy, heart failure, liver disease, and kidney disease, to name just a few.

Regardless of the cause, when blood or other fluid accumulates in the pleural cavity, problems arise. If fluid prevents the lung from expanding properly, shortness of breath can result, as well as a significant decrease in the amount of oxygen that makes it into the bloodstream. The goal in these situations is to reduce the amount of fluid compressing the lung. This might be accomplished by medication, but often it requires drainage of the blood or fluid in the chest.

A pneumothorax occurs when air enters the pleural cavity. This most often results from lung disease, such as emphysema or asthma, but can also be due to malignancy, connective tissue disease, or trauma.

Smoking

If I could suggest two things to help keep you healthy, there would be one "do" and one "don't."

First, DO exercise regularly. Exercise helps you feel better. It increases your endurance. It is good for the health of your heart and lungs. Many people say that they even concentrate better when they are exercising regularly. You don't have to run a marathon every week. Just get off the couch, get out from behind your computer, and get active!

Now for the DON'T. Never, ever, ever, under any circumstances, start smoking. There is absolutely nothing positive about smoking. It's not good for you. It's not cool (no matter what some people might say!). It makes your breath and clothes smell bad. It costs money (which then just goes up in smoke). And it can damage your body in ways that time can never undo. Let me repeat, just DON'T!

Smoking is one of the leading causes of death worldwide. Estimates place the number of smoking-related deaths in the United States at about 500,000 per year. Compared to nonsmokers, the life expectancy of smokers is reduced by about 13 years. If you stopped reading right here, that statistic alone should be enough to discourage you from ever taking up this terrible habit! In a nonsmoker, the risk of dying of lung cancer is 1 percent. The risk of dying of lung cancer is around 20 percent for a male who smokes and around 12 percent for a female who smokes. And although lung cancer is very, very serious, it's not only thing related to smoking.

Smoking increases the risk of heart attack, peripheral vascular disease, cancer of the larynx and mouth, emphysema, pancreatic cancer, bladder cancer, and stomach cancer. I honestly cannot think of a single positive thing when it comes to smoking. Let me repeat, just DON'T!

I would conclude this section with a painful personal note. My own mother died in her early 50s. She died of lung cancer. She was a two-pack-per-day smoker. Before she died, she begged her grandchildren to always remember what she went through as a direct result of smoking. She told them never to be so foolish as to start.

Just DON'T!

Healthy lungs

Smoking and Emphysema

Emphysema

Healthy alveoli

Large air cavity lined with carbon deposits formed

Harmful particles trapped in alveoli

Inflammatory response triggered

Inflammatory chemicals dissolve alveolar septum

HOW WE BREATHE

We breathe in. We breathe out. We do this on average 12 to 16 times a minute. Although we can consciously decide to take a breath, to breathe faster or slower, to hold our breath, or to take an extra-deep breath, the vast majority of the time we breathe without giving it a thought. And that's a good thing too! Right? Just imagine trying to get some sleep if you had to think about every breath.

So it's automatic when we need it to be, and yet we can have control when we want it. Our Creator thought of everything.

Now that we have examined the parts of the respiratory system, let's take a close look at how we breathe.

Breathing Basics

At first glance, breathing doesn't seem all that complicated. It has only two parts — in and out.

The first phase of breathing is called *inspiration* (or *inhalation*), when air is taken into the lungs. The second phase is called *expiration* (or *exhalation*), when air flows back out of the lungs. Air goes in, air goes out. Nothing to it.

But when you look closer at "how" and "why" the air moves the way it does, you begin to see the wonderful complexity. It's not simple at all.

We will begin by seeing how we get air in. (We'll get it back out later...)

Inspiration

Taking air into the lungs is known as inspiration. It is also called inhalation, inhaling, or just "breathing in." It is such a familiar thing, isn't it? You expand your chest and you feel the air move through your nose and down into your lungs.

Here is how it works.

Recall our discussion about blood flow. How does blood flow? It flows from higher pressure to lower pressure. The higher pressure in the larger arteries causes blood to flow to the smaller, lower pressure arteries downstream.

Air flow works pretty much the same way. Air moves from areas of higher pressure to areas of lower pressure. When the lungs expand or contract, the pressure in the airways changes. This results in air flowing into and out of the lungs.

Imagine the lungs at rest in the thoracic cavity. No inspiration or expiration happening. No pressure changes are occurring. No air is moving.

Now let's take a breath.

Inspiration begins with the contraction of the inspiratory muscles, the *diaphragm* and the intercostal muscles. The diaphragm is the large, dome-shaped muscle located below the lungs. The bases of the lungs rest on the diaphragm. When the diaphragm contracts, it flattens and loses much of its domed shape. As it contracts and flattens, the height of the thoracic cavity increases, making the space in the chest much larger. Air rushes into the enlarged thoracic cavity. Contraction of the diaphragm accounts for about 75 percent of the air movement in a typical breath.

The *intercostal muscles* are the muscles between the ribs. When these muscles contract, they elevate each

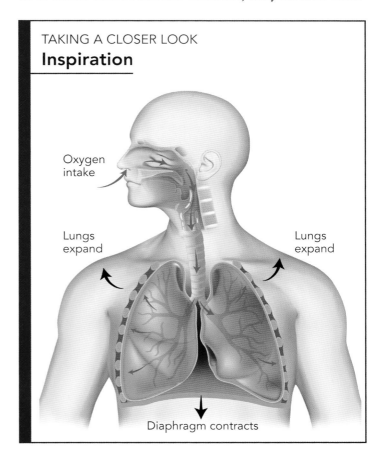

TAKING A CLOSER LOOK
Inspiration

Oxygen intake

Lungs expand

Lungs expand

Diaphragm contracts

rib like the handle on a bucket. This movement of the ribs causes an increase in the size of the thoracic cavity, not only front to back (anteroposteriorly) but also side to side (laterally). The reason for this has to do with how the ribcage was designed. The ribs are attached posteriorly to the vertebral bones and anteriorly to the sternum. When the intercostal muscles contract, the ribs move much in the same way that a bucket handle moves when it is lifted. It moves both up and out at the same time. About 25 percent of the air movement in a basic breath is due to intercostal muscle movement.

As the thoracic cavity enlarges, each lung expands. This happens because the pleura help the lungs "stick" to the chest wall. The parietal pleura is in contact with the chest wall and moves outward with it. Because there is a lot of surface tension between the parietal and visceral pleura, the visceral pleura and the attached lung expand too.

When the diaphragm and intercostal muscles contract, the thoracic cavity expands. As the thoracic cavity expands, the lungs expand as do the airways in the lungs. This lung expansion causes a decrease in the air pressure in the alveoli. When the pressure in the alveoli drops below the pressure in the surrounding environment (atmospheric pressure), air moves into the lungs. This is a simple inspiration.

In some circumstances, when a deeper or more forceful breath is required, there are so-called accessory muscles that come into play. These muscles are not important during normal inspiration, but are used, for example, during exercise. These accessory muscles include the sternocleidomastoid muscles, the scalene muscles, and the pectoralis minor muscles.

Expiration

Getting air back out of the lungs is called expiration, also known as exhalation, exhaling, or "breathing out."

Isn't expiration just the opposite of inspiration? That seems reasonable, but there is a significant difference. You see, expiration is not ordinarily an active process. It is a passive process.

At the end of inspiration, the diaphragm and intercostal muscles simply relax. As they relax, the diaphragm and ribs return to their original position. In addition, due to their natural elasticity, the lungs contract back to their original shape. As this recoil/relaxation takes place, the air pressure in the alveoli increases. When the pressure in the alveoli increases above the pressure in the surrounding environment, air moves out of the lungs. This is a simple expiration. As you see, no active muscle contraction is needed for breathing out.

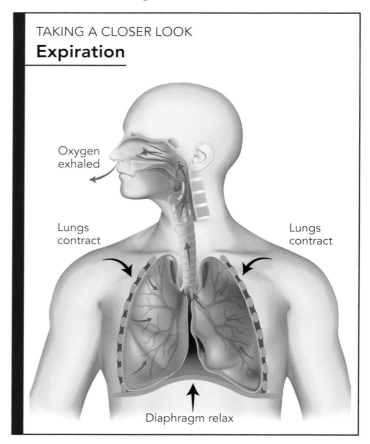

TAKING A CLOSER LOOK
Expiration

Oxygen exhaled

Lungs contract

Lungs contract

Diaphragm relax

There are times when we need a more forceful expiration, like when you are blowing up a balloon or playing the trumpet. In these situations, the abdominal wall muscles can assist expiration by contracting and pushing the abdominal organs upward against the diaphragm. The internal intercostal muscles can also help by pulling the rib cage downward.

Lung Volumes

The *total lung capacity* of an average male is around 6 liters. This is the total amount of air in the lungs at the end of a deep inspiration. We do not, however, move nearly that much air with each breath.

In an adult, a normal breath moves about 500 mL of air into the lungs during inspiration and back out during expiration. This is called the *tidal volume*. The tidal volume is the amount of air in one breath.

Fortunately, we do have the capacity to take in far more than just 500 mL of air in a breath. During heavy exertion we need to take in much more

oxygen. We have a great deal of lung capacity in reserve. To see this for yourself, try this: take a normal breath, and stop. Don't exhale. Now start breathing in again. Breathe as deep as you can. The amount of air taken in *beyond* the normal tidal volume is called the *inspiratory reserve volume*.

Now again, take the deepest breath you can. Hold it for a second or two and then exhale as much air as you can. The amount of air you just exhaled is called the *vital capacity*. This is the maximum amount of air that can be exhaled after a maximum inspiration.

Now if you exhale as completely as possible, can you get all the air out of your lungs? Of course not. And it's a good thing too. There needs to be some air left in the lungs at the end of expiration or the alveoli in the lungs would collapse. The amount of air that remains in the lungs after a maximum expiration is called the *residual volume*.

The amount of air that is moved into and out of the lungs in one minute is called the *minute ventilation*.

TAKING A CLOSER LOOK
Lung Volume

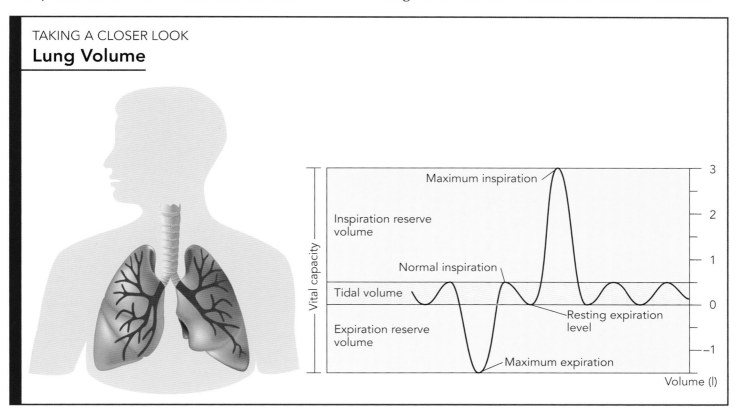

It is easy to calculate. If a person at rest has a tidal volume of 500 mL and breathes 14 times a minute, what do you think the minute ventilation is?

500 mL/breath X 14 breaths/minute

7000 mL/minute

Minute ventilation = 7 liters/minute

This is a calculation of minute ventilation at rest. During exertion, the minute ventilation will be much, much higher.

One other measurement that is often quite helpful is called the *forced expiratory volume in 1 second* (or *FEV₁*). This is, as it would seem, the amount of air that can be forced out of the lungs in one second after a maximal inhalation. Patients with asthma or chronic obstructive pulmonary disease (COPD) often have an abnormal *FEV₁* and its assessment can be helpful in treating those patients.

Gas Exchange

The ultimate purpose of the respiratory system is to get oxygen into the bloodstream so that it can be delivered to the body's tissues and to remove the carbon dioxide generated by the body tissues and expel it from the body. Even as incredible as the anatomy of the respiratory system is, it would be a very poor design if it didn't accomplish its mission. But it does work. It works very well indeed!

Oxygenated blood is pumped from the left ventricle out to the body. When its gets to the capillary beds, the oxygen in the blood moves into the tissues where it is used in metabolic processes. As a consequence of these metabolic activities, carbon dioxide is produced. Carbon dioxide is a waste product and would do serious harm to cells if it were allowed to accumulate. Fortunately, the carbon dioxide that is produced in the tissues moves into the blood in the capillaries to be taken away and disposed of.

The blood leaving the capillary beds has a lower oxygen content than the blood entering the capillary beds. This blood is said to be deoxygenated.

Deoxygenated blood returns to the right atrium and is sent to the right ventricle. The right ventricle pumps the deoxygenated blood to the lungs via the pulmonary artery. This blood makes its way to the capillary beds adjacent to alveoli in the lungs.

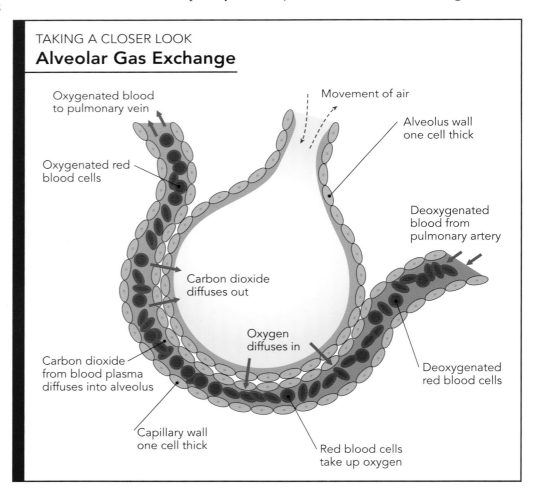

TAKING A CLOSER LOOK
Alveolar Gas Exchange

Oxygenated blood to pulmonary vein

Movement of air

Alveolus wall one cell thick

Oxygenated red blood cells

Deoxygenated blood from pulmonary artery

Carbon dioxide diffuses out

Oxygen diffuses in

Carbon dioxide from blood plasma diffuses into alveolus

Deoxygenated red blood cells

Capillary wall one cell thick

Red blood cells take up oxygen

The alveolus, as we said before, is where gas exchange takes place, and this is the ideal place for this process to occur. The very thin wall of the alveolar cell, adjacent to the thin wall of the capillary, makes a perfect environment to promote the movement of gases into and out of the blood.

After all, it makes sense that it's easier for gases to diffuse through something thin than something thick, right? That is why there is no gas exchange farther back up the bronchial tree. Those structures (bronchi and bronchioles) are too thick to allow for proper gas exchange. The alveoli are perfectly designed for gas exchange.

The total surface area for gas exchange provided by the alveoli is staggering! With at least 300 million alveoli in our lungs, if you spread all the alveoli out on a flat surface, it would cover an area a little more than 750 square feet! That is a lot of area for gases to diffuse through. This is another evidence of the amazing design of the human body. It didn't just happen by accident.

Oxygen Transport

Step one of gas exchange is to get the oxygen in the alveoli into the blood in the alveolar capillaries. In other words, the "deoxygenated" blood needs to be "oxygenated." Seems simple, but how does it work?

Well, doesn't the oxygen in the alveoli just move into the blood on its own? After all, we said these membranes were thin enough for the oxygen to move through them easily. That's true enough, but as usual, there's more to it than that.

When oxygen reaches the blood in the capillaries, it doesn't just dissolve in the blood plasma and get carried away to the tissues. In fact, when you look closely, you will find that blood plasma does not make a very good carrier of oxygen. You see, oxygen does not dissolve well in water. Blood plasma only

carries about 2 percent of the oxygen found in the bloodstream — so there must be something else in the blood to "do the heavy lifting," so to speak. There must be something in the blood that can carry oxygen efficiently. And that thing is called hemoglobin.

The erythrocytes (red blood cells) in the blood contain a protein called hemoglobin. Hemoglobin is composed of four polypeptide chains and four heme groups. Each of the four heme groups contains an iron atom. Each iron atom in the hemoglobin molecule can bind to one oxygen molecule, so every hemoglobin molecule can bind with a maximum of four oxygen molecules.

Hemoglobin binds oxygen molecules very efficiently, and the vast majority of the oxygen in the blood (98 percent or so) is bound to hemoglobin. When hemoglobin is bound to one or more oxygen molecules, it is called *oxyhemoglobin*. When the hemoglobin is not bound to any oxygen molecules, it is called *deoxyhemoglobin*.

When four molecules of oxygen are bound, the oxyhemoglobin is "fully saturated." If one, two, or

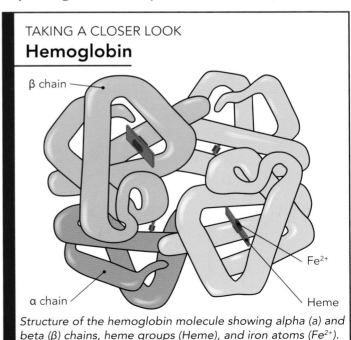

TAKING A CLOSER LOOK
Hemoglobin

β chain

Fe^{2+}

α chain

Heme

Structure of the hemoglobin molecule showing alpha (a) and beta (β) chains, heme groups (Heme), and iron atoms (Fe^{2+}).

three oxygen molecules are bound, the oxyhemoglobin is only "partially saturated."

The presence of hemoglobin is the reason that our blood is red. Oxyhemoglobin is bright red in color. Deoxyhemoglobin is a much duller shade of red. This is why arterial blood (oxygenated) looks redder than venous (deoxygenated) blood.

Each red blood cell contains around 270 million hemoglobin molecules. So, at maximum saturation, every red blood cell can carry one billion oxygen molecules! That's a LOT of oxygen molecules.

Oxygen contained in inspired air is delivered to the alveoli, and it moves into the alveolar capillaries where it binds to hemoglobin. In yet another testimony to our Creator, hemoglobin has an incredible property. After the first oxygen molecule binds to hemoglobin, the hemoglobin molecule alters its shape slightly to enhance the binding of other oxygen molecules! (No way that happened by chance. Our Creator thought of everything!) This is a very efficient system.

The now-oxygenated blood is carried back to the left side of the heart by the pulmonary veins. The left side of the heart then sends it out to the body's tissues. Upon arrival in the capillary beds of the body's tissues, the oxygenated blood finds itself in an entirely different situation. Whereas in the alveoli the oxygen level was relatively high, oxygen levels in the tissues surrounding the capillaries are relatively low. So what happens to the oxyhemoglobin

Carbon Monoxide Poisoning

Carbon monoxide is a colorless, odorless gas that consists of one carbon atom and one oxygen atom. It is generated by the burning of carbon-based substances like wood, coal, and gasoline.

People can be poisoned by exposure to carbon monoxide, and a number of deaths are caused each year by this type of poisoning. This can occur when combustion of things like wood or gasoline takes place in poorly ventilated areas. In circumstances like these, people may not realize they are being exposed until significant symptoms develop. Symptoms can include headache, shortness of breath, and nausea. If exposure continues, more severe symptoms can follow, such as confusion, vomiting, and loss of consciousness. In the worst cases, death can occur.

Many homes contain carbon monoxide detectors to alert sleeping people about carbon monoxide leaks in the home. Since carbon monoxide poisoning makes people sleepy, people would not awaken to save themselves without this sort of warning. In a house with a carbon monoxide furnace leak, such a detector can save the lives of everyone in the home.

Carbon monoxide binds very effectively to hemoglobin. In fact, it binds to hemoglobin much more efficiently than oxygen. Carbon monoxide is particularly dangerous because it competes with oxygen for binding sites in the heme group. Plus, hemoglobin's binding to carbon monoxide is 200 times greater than for oxygen.

People exposed to carbon monoxide require prompt medical attention. Treatment for those patients is therapy with 100 percent oxygen until the carbon monoxide clears from the body.

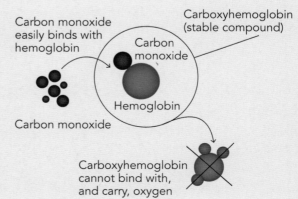

Carbon monoxide easily binds with hemoglobin

Carboxyhemoglobin (stable compound)

Carbon monoxide

Hemoglobin

Carbon monoxide

Carboxyhemoglobin cannot bind with, and carry, oxygen

here? If you think it now releases its bound oxygen molecules, you are correct! The released oxygen molecules then move out of the capillaries and enter the body tissue cells where they are needed.

As efficiently as it binds oxygen in conditions of high oxygen concentration, hemoglobin is equally efficient at releasing its oxygen when the surrounding oxygen levels are low. Even at that, not all the oxygen is released from all the hemoglobin molecules in the systemic capillaries. That would not work well at all. Here's why.

When we are at rest, the hemoglobin is almost completely saturated. In fact, it is around 98 percent saturated. That means the hemoglobin in oxygenated blood carries 98 percent of the maximum amount of oxygen it could theoretically hold. After the blood passes through the systemic capillaries we call it "deoxygenated," yet the hemoglobin is still 70 to 75 percent saturated! You see, the hemoglobin doesn't give up all its oxygen on every trip through the body. There's still plenty in reserve. And that's as it should be.

Under normal conditions while at rest, the body only uses about 25 percent of the available oxygen in the blood. But we are not always at rest, are we? During periods of exertion, the body's tissues need much more oxygen to meet their metabolic needs. In situations like this, the body is able to obtain a higher percentage of the oxygen bound to the hemoglobin than it does at rest. But wait a minute, how does hemoglobin release more oxygen at some times and less at others? Hemoglobin can't "know" anything. It doesn't "know" when someone is exercising. It's merely a molecule in the blood. The answer is that there are conditions in the body itself that can cause hemoglobin to release oxygen more readily.

First of all, tissues that are metabolically very active, such as muscles during exertion, can produce acids as a byproduct of that activity. As a result, the acidity of the blood in the region near these tissues increases. Tissues at rest produce far less of these substances, and thus the acid level in the blood near resting tissues is lower. Hemoglobin releases oxygen more readily in a more acidic environment. So the higher the tissue activity, the higher the acidity near these tissues, and ultimately, the more oxygen released to these active tissues.

Second, active tissues produce more carbon dioxide than tissues at rest. Carbon dioxide also binds to hemoglobin, and when it does, it causes the hemoglobin to unload its oxygen more easily. So again, the conditions near active tissues induce hemoglobin to give up its oxygen.

Third, higher temperatures cause hemoglobin to release oxygen. Again, this is another of the conditions found near active tissues. The more active the tissues are, the more heat is generated, and then, the higher the temperature in the capillary beds serving these tissues. So once again, here is a condition expected near tissues requiring more oxygen that leads to more oxygen being released.

It seems almost unfair to say that the respiratory system is designed to deliver oxygen to the tissues. It is really over-designed when you think about it. There are so many features working so well together: the design of the alveoli, the hemoglobin molecule itself, and the ability of hemoglobin to alter its binding to oxygen in response to the precise conditions produced by active tissues. It makes no sense to think these things could all be some sort of chemical accident occurring over millions of years.

The entire process of oxygen delivery speaks to the abilities of the Master Designer.

Carbon Dioxide Transport

Not only does the respiratory system take oxygen to the tissues, it has to remove the carbon dioxide produced by these same tissues. There are three main ways that carbon dioxide is carried by the blood.

Carbon dioxide can dissolve in the blood plasma. It dissolves in plasma much better than oxygen does. About 10 percent of the carbon dioxide in the blood is carried in this fashion.

Hemoglobin not only transports oxygen, it can also transport carbon dioxide. However, the carbon

The Placenta

We mentioned earlier that a baby in the womb does not have to use its lungs to breathe. Yet a baby of course needs to get oxygen into his or her blood cells and to release carbon dioxide to be carried away. God designed a wonderful way for a baby's gas exchange to take place. He designed a placenta. In the placenta, the mother's blood flows through capillaries right next to capillaries containing the baby's blood. The baby's blood is carried there in the umbilical cord and, once oxygenated, returns to the baby the same way. The mother's and baby's blood do not mix. Instead, oxygen is released from the hemoglobin in the mother's red blood cells. The oxygen crosses from the capillaries containing the mother's blood into the capillaries containing the baby's blood. There, the baby's hemoglobin molecules grab the oxygen molecules and carry it back to the baby.

You might wonder, since the mother's and the baby's blood both contain hemoglobin, how the mother's hemoglobin "knows" to release oxygen for the baby's hemoglobin to pick up. Here God designed a particularly wonderful system. He made a special kind of hemoglobin just for unborn babies. Fetal hemoglobin has an even greater affinity (attraction) for oxygen than ordinary hemoglobin. The unborn baby's hemoglobin is able to overcome the attraction of the mother's hemoglobin and carry away all the oxygen the baby needs from the placenta. Once a baby is born, red blood cells begin to be made with adult hemoglobin, and generally by about six months of age the fetal hemoglobin has been replaced.

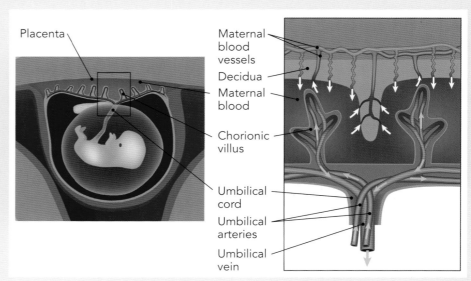

Placenta

Maternal blood vessels

Decidua

Maternal blood

Chorionic villus

Umbilical cord

Umbilical arteries

Umbilical vein

dioxide carried by hemoglobin is not bound to iron but instead is attached to amino acids. These amino acids are part of the polypeptide chains that make up the globin part of hemoglobin. When hemoglobin is carrying carbon dioxide it is called *carbaminohemoglobin*. Approximately 20 percent of the carbon dioxide in the blood is transported by hemoglobin.

The remaining 70 percent of the carbon dioxide is transported in the blood plasma as bicarbonate ions (HCO_3.). After carbon dioxide enters the plasma, it soon finds its way to the red blood cells. Once inside the RBC, the carbon dioxide combines with water and is turned into carbonic acid. This reaction occurs very rapidly due to the presence of a special enzyme called *carbonic anhydrase*. The carbonic acid quickly breaks down into a hydrogen ion and a bicarbonate ion. The bicarbonate ion is the form in which the carbon dioxide is carried to the lungs.

In the systemic capillaries where the carbon dioxide levels are high, the tendency is for more carbonic acid to be produced and then, ultimately, more bicarbonate ions. The bicarbonate ions are then carried to the lungs by the blood. In the lungs, the levels of carbon dioxide are relatively low, so the reaction here is reversed. The bicarbonate combines with the hydrogen ions to again form carbonic acid. Then, with the help of the carbonic anhydrase enzyme, the carbonic acid is broken down into carbon dioxide and water. The carbon dioxide then diffuses out of the blood and into the alveoli. It is then taken away with the expired air!

Control of Respiration

We breathe in and out, in and out. Thousands of times a day. And we really never give it a thought. It just happens. Automatically.

But stop and think a minute. We do have control over our breathing — a lot of control when we need it. If we didn't have the ability to voluntarily hold our breath, we could not go swimming. If we could not precisely control our respiratory system on command, we would not be able to talk or shout or sing.

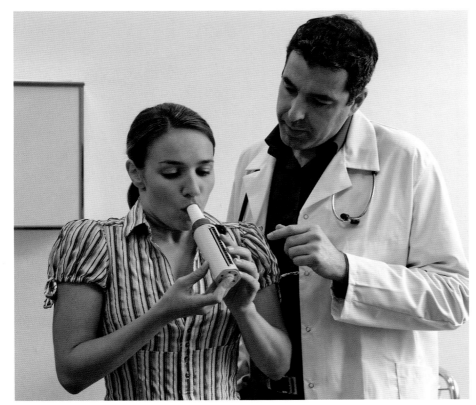

The respiratory system has both voluntary and involuntary controls. And that's a very, very good thing.

The primary control of respiration takes place in the brain, in the medulla oblongata. There are two locations in the medulla that make up what is known as the medullary respiratory center. The first of these is the ventral respiratory group (VRG), and the second is the dorsal respiratory group (DRG). From these two centers, nerve signals are sent to the intercostal muscles and the diaphragm to stimulate them to contract. The contraction of these muscles (as you should recall) triggers inspiration. These impulses are generated for about two seconds, and then they cease. When the nerve signals stop, the intercostal muscles and the diaphragm relax. The natural recoil of these structures leads to expiration. Remember, expiration is generally a passive process. The cessation of nerve stimulation lasts 2–3 seconds, and then stimulation occurs again.

Inspiration is triggered by impulses from both the VRG and the DRG. However, the VRG does have another function. There are times when more forceful expirations are needed. In these circumstances, the VRG sends nerve impulses to the internal intercostal muscles and the muscles of the abdominal wall. Contraction of these muscles helps decrease the size of the thoracic cavity and assists with a forceful expiration.

Another important area is the pneumotaxic area located in the pons. It is sometimes referred to as the pontine respiratory group (PRG). The pneumotaxic area coordinates the switch between inspiration and expiration. The PRG helps regulate how much air is taken in with each breath. It can send signals to turn off the VRG and DRG to help limit inspiration. This can keep the lungs from getting too full of air.

The operation of the respiratory centers is regulated by many inputs from the body.

First of all, we do have significant voluntary control over the respiratory system. This is possible because there are nerve pathways connecting the cerebral cortex to the respiratory centers. This gives us the ability to alter our inspiration and expiration. Of course, this control is within limits. For example, we cannot hold our breath for extended periods of time. Usually, after a minute or so, involuntary control of the respiratory system takes over and causes us to breathe whether we want to or not. These involuntary controls help protect the body and maintain proper levels of oxygen and carbon dioxide.

Further control of the respiratory system is based on input from special sensory cells called chemoreceptors. These special cells are sensitive to changes in the levels of certain chemicals or substances in the body. There are two main groups of chemoreceptors that regulate the respiratory system — the central chemoreceptors that are located in the brain stem, and the peripheral chemoreceptors found in the arch of the aorta and the carotid arteries. These cells help monitor blood levels of oxygen and carbon dioxide, as well as the acidity of the blood itself.

What is the most important thing that the respiratory system does? If you said that taking in oxygen and getting it into the bloodstream is most

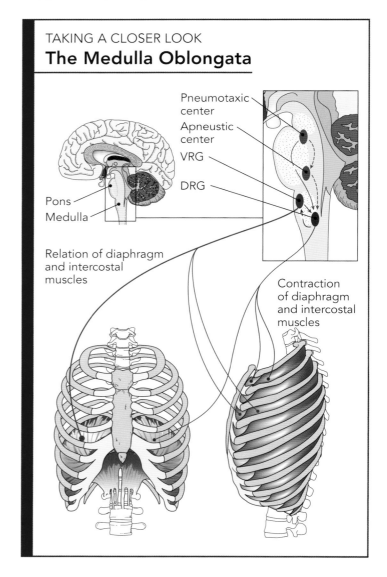

TAKING A CLOSER LOOK
The Medulla Oblongata

Pneumotaxic center
Apneustic center
VRG
DRG
Pons
Medulla
Relation of diaphragm and intercostal muscles
Contraction of diaphragm and intercostal muscles

important, you would be correct. Oxygen is the most important thing. A person can live only a few minutes without oxygen, so it is vital to keeping our bodies alive.

From this fact, you probably would assume that the primary thing that the chemoreceptors monitor is oxygen, right? Well, as it happens, that's not the case. The chemical in the body that has the most influence on respiration is actually carbon dioxide, not oxygen! And this makes sense when you give it some thought. Recall that the body uses only about 25 percent of the oxygen bound by hemoglobin, so under normal circumstances, there is plenty of oxygen in reserve. If the chemoreceptors primarily checked for oxygen, then we would have little stimulus to breathe because there is always so much oxygen in the blood. Our brains wouldn't signal the need to breathe until we were nearly out of oxygen with no reserve. If mindless evolutionary processes "designed" us we might have been made that way, but God is far wiser. He designed us to breathe before we become in desperate need of oxygen to survive.

It makes much more sense to monitor the levels of carbon dioxide, and this is what the central chemoreceptors do. They monitor the levels of carbon dioxide (in addition to monitoring the acidity of the blood). When the receptors sense the levels of carbon dioxide going up, what do you think happens? Correct! The chemoreceptors send signals to the respiratory center to increase respiration and remove the excess carbon dioxide. The opposite occurs when the level of carbon dioxide gets a little too low. The chemoreceptors trigger the respiratory center to slow respiration and allow the carbon dioxide level to return to normal. This control mechanism is very precise. It not only maintains control of the respiratory system, it also helps keep the level of carbon dioxide within very tight limits.

The level of acidity in the blood is also monitored by the central chemoreceptors. An increase in acid

levels is usually accompanied by an increase in respiration.

While oxygen is not the primary controller of respiration, its level is also monitored by chemoreceptors. The peripheral chemoreceptors keep a close watch on the oxygen level in the blood. However, the oxygen level has to get very low before the peripheral chemoreceptors trigger an increase in respiration. It is very unusual for the peripheral chemoreceptors to be the primary stimulus for respiration.

3

IS THIS "DESIGN" JUST AN ACCIDENT?

We have explored the wonderful complexities of the cardiovascular and respiratory systems. I promise there is much, much more to come. In the other volumes of *Wonders of the Human Body* we will look further into the amazing creation that is the human body. The secrets of the nervous system, the digestive system, the endocrine system, skin, blood, and more await you.

The design of the body seems obvious at every turn. But not to everyone it seems. You see, many people would have you believe that the marvelous complexity of the body is merely the result of chance. They want you to believe that the body came into existence by means of a process called "evolution." The basis of this belief is that billions of years ago, matter just appeared. Out of nothing. From nowhere. Then the chemicals in the universe proceeded to form stars, planets, and galaxies. On their own. Without direction.

And then...

These chemicals randomly bouncing off one another formed our sun and the planets in the solar system, including, of course, the earth. In the earth's vast oceans, chemicals continued to bang together, and somehow the first living cell formed. By itself. Without direction. By chance.

Over the next three billion years or so, this one-celled organism became more and more complex, and new types of living things came into existence. More and more complex creatures evolved. By chance. On their own.

Next, there arose an ape-like creature that is said to be our ancestor. Over the last few million years this ape-like ancestor evolved into both the modern apes and humans. By chance. On its own. Without direction.

To those who accept evolution, the incredibly complex machine that is the human body is the result of random chance processes. Ultimately, the body is just a cosmic accident. Nothing marvelous about it at all. Just a cosmic accident.

Curious...

You might perhaps be asking yourself just where all the matter in the universe came from in the first place. Excellent question. The evolutionist has no answer. Maybe you are wondering where all the information came from to allow a one-celled organism to increase in complexity, that increase in complexity resulting in human beings. Another excellent question. Again, the evolutionist has no answer.

I have an answer, and it's painfully simple. Evolution didn't happen. Period.

There is no way that the complexity in our world can merely be written off as the result of chance. Whether it's a simple one-celled organism (actually to suggest that one-celled organisms are simple is ridiculous; they are extremely complex), a jellyfish, a flower, a butterfly, or a giraffe, everything in our world is obviously the work of a Master Designer. One would have to suspend reality to believe that these complex things "just happened."

The Word of God refers to how the amazing things that God made should direct a person's attention to his or her Creator. Romans 1:20–22 tells us:

For since the creation of the world His invisible attributes are clearly seen, being understood by the things that are made, even His eternal power and Godhead, so that they are without excuse, because, although they knew God, they did not glorify Him as God, nor were thankful, but became futile in their thoughts, and their foolish hearts were darkened. Professing to be wise, they became fools.

As you explore and consider the human body, I pray you will not lose sight of the greatest wonder of all: the awesome power of Jesus Christ, our Creator and Savior.

He is indeed the Master Designer. As we read in Colossians 1:16–17:

For by Him all things were created that are in heaven and that are on earth, visible and invisible, whether thrones or dominions or principalities or powers. All things were created through Him and for Him. And He is before all things, and in Him all things consist.

Let us praise Him for the great things He has done!

4

THE GOSPEL

As incredible as our bodies are, they do not last forever. Eventually, they wear out or become damaged from disease or injury. But why is that exactly? If the body is so amazing, why do we die?

God's Word gives us the answer to this question.

In the beginning God created everything. He created everything is six days. He made the first man, Adam, and the first woman, Eve. They were created in the image of God.

So God created man in His own image; in the image of God He created him; male and female He created them (Genesis 1:27).

Creation

Sin and death

Redemption

Resurrection

After He finished creating, He looked on all He had made and called it "very good." It was a perfect world where there was no death. And in the perfect world, God gave man a choice, obey Me or disobey Me.

And the LORD God commanded the man, saying, "Of every tree of the garden you may freely eat; but of the tree of the knowledge of good and evil you shall not eat, for in the day that you eat of it you shall surely die" (Genesis 2:16–17).

Unfortunately, man chose to disobey God.

So when the woman saw that the tree was good for food, that it was pleasant to the eyes, and a tree desirable to make one wise, she took of its fruit and ate. She also gave to her husband with her, and he ate (Genesis 3:6).

Man's rebellion brought death and corrupted God's perfect creation. Because of man's sin, death became a part of this world and has been ever since.

But God had a plan. He had a plan to defeat death. A plan that would give us the opportunity to be with Him forever in heaven after we die. He sent His Son, the Lord Jesus Christ, to walk this earth as a man. Jesus Christ lived a sinless life so that He could take the punishment that is rightfully ours. He did this when He was crucified, dying on a cross. Then three days later He came back to life, forever defeating death and purchasing for all who trust in Him a life in heaven forever.

For God so loved the world that He gave His only begotten Son, that whoever believes in Him should not perish but have everlasting life (John 3:16).

But how can we have everlasting life? We are not worthy of it! God's Word tells us that we are all sinners and therefore deserve to die.

. . . for all have sinned and fall short of the glory of God (Romans 3:23).

. . . the wages of sin is death, but the gift of God is eternal life in Christ Jesus our Lord (Romans 6:23).

Eventually, our bodies will die, but we can defeat death. Not physical death, but spiritual death. You see, physical death is not the end. We all have souls that will live on into eternity. The choice we have to make is where we will spend eternity, with God or apart from Him forever.

Each of us will die physically and then be judged. But if we have trusted in Christ, we have nothing to fear. Jesus already paid the price for our sins!

And as it is appointed for men to die once, but after this the judgment, so Christ was offered once to bear the sins of many. . . (Hebrews 9:27–28).

God promises that all who, repenting of their sins, trust in Jesus, will be saved.

. . . that if you confess with your mouth the Lord Jesus and believe in your heart that God has raised Him from the dead, you will be saved (Romans 10:9).

Where will you spend eternity — with God or apart from Him?

GLOSSARY

alveoli — the plural of alveolus.

alveolus — microscopic air sac that is the endpoint of the respiratory system. It is the site of gas exchange between the air and the blood and the alveolar capillaries.

anatomy — the study of the body's parts and how they are put together.

aorta — the largest artery in the body. The aorta carries blood from the left ventricle into the systemic circulation (out to the body's tissues).

aortic valve — the valve between the left ventricle and the aorta. Blood flows from the left ventricle through the aortic valve into the aorta.

arterioles — the smallest arteries. Arterioles lead into the capillaries.

artery — vessel that carries blood away from the heart.

atrioventricular bundle (Bundle of His) — the portion of the cardiac conduction system that conducts the signal from the AV node to the inter-ventricular septum.

atrioventricular node (AV node) — the portion of the cardiac conduction system that is the first step in sending the signal to the ventricles. In the AV node, the signal is delayed approximately 0.1 second to allow the atria to complete their contraction before the ventricles contract.

autorhythmic cells — special cardiac cells that can generate electrical impulses without any outside stimulus.

baroreceptor — special sensory cells found primarily in the aorta and larger arteries. The cells are sensitive to being stretched, thus they are ideal for detecting changes in blood pressure.

blood pressure — the pressure of blood inside a blood vessel.

bradycardia — a heart rate less than 60 beats per minute.

bronchi — the main passageways of air into the lungs. The trachea branches to form the right and left bronchi.

bronchiole — smaller branches of the bronchial tree that do not have cartilage in their walls.

capillary — the smallest kind of blood vessel in the body. The wall of a capillary consists of a single layer of endothelial cells.

carbonic anhydrase — an enzyme that accelerates the conversion of water and carbon dioxide into carbonic acid. It also assists with the conversion of carbonic acid back into water and carbon dioxide.

cardiac cycle — the steps involved in filling the heart's chambers and pumping the blood.

cardiac muscle — one of the three types of muscle. The myocardium is composed primarily of cardiac muscle.

cardiac output — the amount of blood pumped by the heart in one minute.

cardiac reserve — the difference between the cardiac output at rest and cardiac output during maximal exertion.

cardiac tamponade — a serious medical condition is which the pericardial sac has accumulated so much fluid that the heart cannot squeeze properly.

cell — the most basic structural and functional unit of a living organism, such as the human body. A cell generally consists of three parts: the nucleus, the cell membrane, and the cytoplasm.

cellular respiration — the process inside cells in which nutrients are metabolized into energy.

chemoreceptor — special cells sensitive to changes in the levels of certain chemicals or substances in the body.

chordae tendineae — bands of fibrous tissue that connect the papillary muscles in the ventricles to the tricuspid and mitral valves. These bands help prevent the valves from being pushed backward into the atria during ventricular systole.

cilia — tiny hairlike structures on cells. These hairs help sweep mucus and debris out of the respiratory system.

contractility — how hard the cardiac muscle can contract when it is stretched to a certain point.

deoxyhemoglobin — hemoglobin that is not bound to any oxygen molecules.

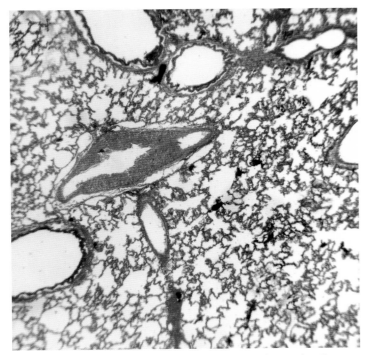

Normal Lung Tissue. The larger holes are blood vessels. The smaller spaces are alveoli.

diastole — the period of time when a heart chamber is relaxing.

diastolic blood pressure — the lowest pressure in the arterial system during left ventricular diastole.

dorsal respiratory group (DRG) — a group of specialized cells located in the medulla. Signals are sent from the DRG to the diaphragm and intercostal muscles to stimulate them to contract. This triggers inspiration.

ejection fraction — the percentage of the volume of blood in the left ventricle ejected with each beat. It is normally 60–70%.

end diastolic volume — the amount of blood in the ventricle when it is full (at the end of diastole).

end systolic volume — the amount of blood remaining in the ventricle after it contracts.

endocardium — the inner layer of the heart.

epicardium — the outermost layer of the heart.

epiglottis — a flap made of cartilage located at the entrance of the larynx. When swallowing, the epiglottis closes and prevents food from going into the trachea.

evolution — the belief that everything in the universe arose as the result of random chemical reactions. The stars, the planets, and all living things, including man, are — according to evolutionary thinking — ultimately just chemical accidents that arose over millions and billions of years.

exhalation — the flow of air out of the lungs. It is also called "expiration."

expiration — the flow of air out of the lungs. It is also called "exhalation."

external respiration — the process of moving air from the environment into and out of the lungs.

heart murmur — an abnormal gurgling or rushing sound that occurs as the heart beats. While abnormal, a murmur is not necessarily an indication of heart disease. Many heart murmurs are benign (harmless).

heart rate — the speed at which the heart is beating. It is most often reported as the number of beats per minute.

hemoglobin — an iron-containing protein found in red blood cells. It is involved in the transport of oxygen to the tissues.

hilum — located on the medial surface of the lung. It is where the bronchi and blood vessels enter the lung.

homeostasis — maintaining various processes and conditions within appropriate limits. For example, blood sugar, body temperature, and blood pressure need to be neither too high nor too low. Many home-ostatic mechanisms maintain equilibrium among the body's systems.

hypertension — a blood pressure consistently above 140/90; frequently called "high blood pressure."

inhalation — the flow of air into the lungs. It is also called "inspiration."

inspiration — the flow of air into the lungs. It is also called "inhalation."

internal respiration — the process of exchanging oxygen and carbon dioxide between the environment and the body's cells. It involves gas exchange between the air and the blood in the alveolar capillaries and the gas exchange between the blood in the systemic capillaries and the body's cells.

larynx — the portion of the airway that connects the laryngopharynx to the trachea. It is often called the "voice box."

left ventricle — the chamber of the heart responsible for pumping blood into the systemic circulation.

lower respiratory system — the trachea, the bronchi, and the lungs.

lumen — the inner space of a blood vessel. The blood flows in the lumen of the vessel.

minute ventilation — the amount of air moved into and out of the lungs in one minute.

mitochondria — organelles inside a cell that generate and store energy.

mitral valve — the valve between the left atrium and the left ventricle. Blood flows from the left atrium through the mitral valve into the left ventricle.

myocardium — the middle layer of the heart. It is composed primarily of cardiac muscle.

organ — a group of tissues that have a specific function.

oxyhemoglobin — hemoglobin that is bound to one or more oxygen molecules.

pericarditis — inflammation of the pericardium.

pericardium — the double-walled sac surrounding the heart.

pharynx — the portion of the respiratory system beginning at the rear of the nasal cavity and extending down to the larynx. It is commonly called the "throat."

physiology — the study of how the parts of the body function.

pleura — the double-walled membrane that covers the lungs. It is composed of the visceral pleura and the parietal pleura.

pneumotaxic area — an area of the pons that coordinates the switch between inspiration and expiration. It is also known as the Pontine respiratory group (PRG).

pontine respiratory group (PRG) — an area of the pons that coordinates the switch between inspiration and expiration. It is also known as the pneumatic area.

preload — the amount that cardiac muscle is stretched by the blood in it before contracting.

pulmonary valve — the valve between the right ventricle and the pulmonary artery. Blood flows from the right ventricle through the pulmonary valve into the pulmonary artery.

pulse pressure — the difference between the systolic blood pressure and the diastolic blood pressure.

right ventricle — the chamber of the heart responsible for pumping blood into the pulmonary circulation.

sinoatrial node (SA node) — a group of auto-rhythmic cells in the upper portion of the right atrium. The SA node is the heart's main pacemaker.

stroke volume — the amount of blood pumped with each beat.

surfactant — a detergent-like substance found in alveolar fluid. It helps keep the alveoli from collapsing.

systole — the period of time when a heart chamber is contracting.

systolic blood pressure — the highest pressure reached in the arterial system during left ventricular systole.

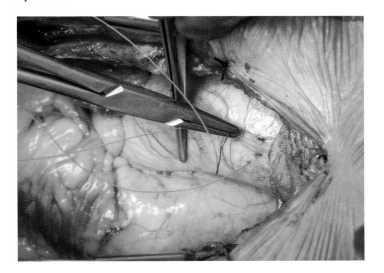

tachycardia — a heart rate greater than 100 beats per minute.

tissue — a group of cells that perform similar or related functions. There are four basic tissue types: epithelial, muscle, connective, and nervous.

tricuspid valve — the valve between the right atrium and the right ventricle. Blood flows from the right atrium through the tricuspid valve into the right ventricle.

tunica externa — the outermost layer of a blood vessel. It is made of collage and elastic fibers.

tunica intima — the innermost layer of a blood vessel. It is composed of a smooth layer of tissue called the endothelium.

tunica media — the middle layer of a blood vessel. It consists mainly of smooth muscle and elastic fibers.

upper respiratory system — the part of the respiratory system above the level of the chest. It includes the nose, nasal cavity, the sinuses, the pharynx, and the larynx.

vasoconstriction — when the lumen of a blood vessel gets smaller. This is the result of contraction of the smooth muscle in the blood vessel. This increases the pressure in the lumen.

vasodilation — when the lumen of a blood vessel gets larger. This is the result of relaxation of the smooth muscle in the blood vessel. This decreases the pressure in the lumen.

vein— vessel that carries blood back to the heart.

ventilation — the movement of air into and out of the lungs by means of inspiration and expiration.

ventral respiratory group (VRG) — a group of specialized cells located in the medulla. Signals are sent from the VRG to the diaphragm and intercostal muscles to stimulate them. The VRG can stimulate both inspiration and forced expiration.

venule — the smallest veins. They carry blood from the capillaries to the larger veins.

INDEX

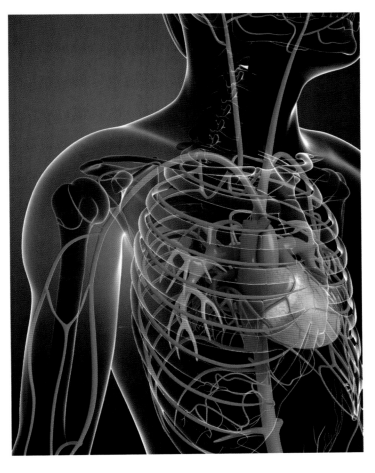

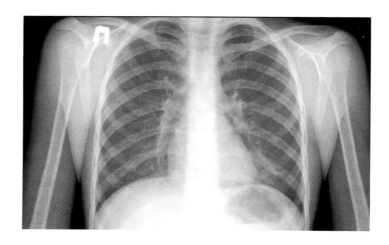

Photo Credits

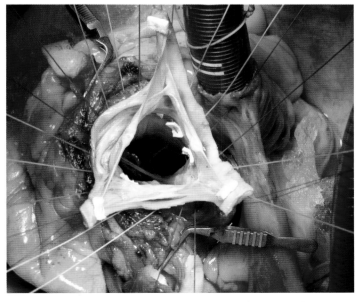

Surgery on an aortic valve to help protect it from possibly rupturing.

DR. TOMMY MITCHELL

Dr. Tommy Mitchell graduated with a BA with highest honors from the University of Tennessee-Knoxville in 1980 with a major in cell biology. For his superior scholarship during his undergraduate study, he was elected to Phi Beta Kappa Society (the oldest and one of the most respected honor societies in America). He subsequently attended Vanderbilt University School of Medicine, where he received his medical degree in 1984.

Dr. Mitchell completed his residency at Vanderbilt University Affiliated Hospitals in 1987. He is Board Certified in Internal Medicine. In 1991, he was elected a Fellow of the American College of Physicians (F.A.C.P.). Tommy had a thriving medical practice in his hometown of Gallatin, Tennessee, for 20 years, but, in late 2006, he withdrew from medical practice to join Answers in Genesis where he presently serves as a full time speaker, writer, and researcher.

As a scientist, physician, and father, Dr. Mitchell has a burden to provide solid answers from the Bible to equip people to stand firm in the face of personal tragedy and popular evolutionary misinformation. Using communication skills developed over many years of medical practice, he is able to connect with people at all educational levels and unveil the truth that can change their lives.

Dr. Mitchell has been married to his wife Elizabeth (herself a retired obstetrician) for over 30 years, and they have three daughters. His hobbies include Martin guitars, anything to do with Bill Monroe (the famous bluegrass musician), and Apple computers. He does also admit to spending an excessive amount of time playing cribbage with Ken Ham.

CREATION BASED

HIGH SCHOOL SCIENCE

WITH LABS

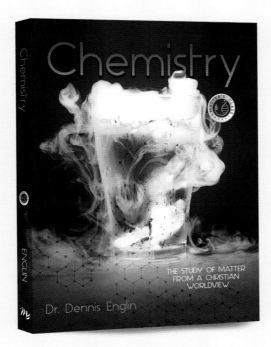

MASTER'S CLASS: CHEMISTRY
GRADE 10-12 | 978-1-68344-134-2

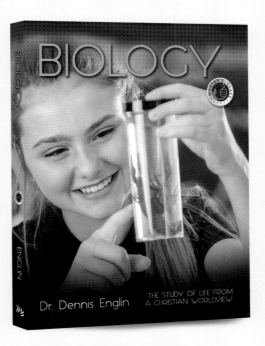

MASTER'S CLASS: BIOLOGY
GRADE 9-12 | 978-1-68344-152-6

JACOBS' MATH

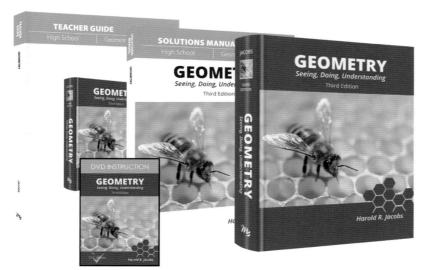

JACOBS' GEOMETRY

An authoritative standard for years, with nearly one million students having learned geometry principles through the text.

Jacobs' Geometry	978-1-68344-020-8
Solutions Manual	978-1-68344-021-5
Teacher Guide	978-1-68344-022-2
3-BOOK SET	**978-1-68344-036-9**
Geometry DVD	713438-10236-8
3-BOOK / 1-DVD SET	**978-1-68344-037-6**

JACOBS' ALGEBRA

This provides a full year of math in a clearly written format with guidance for teachers as well as for students who are self-directed.

Elementary Algebra	978-0-89051-985-1
Solutions Manual	978-0-89051-987-5
Teacher Guide	978-0-89051-986-8
3-BOOK SET	**978-0-89051-988-2**
Elementary Algebra DVD	713438-10237-5
3-BOOK / 1-DVD SET	**978-1-68344-038-3**

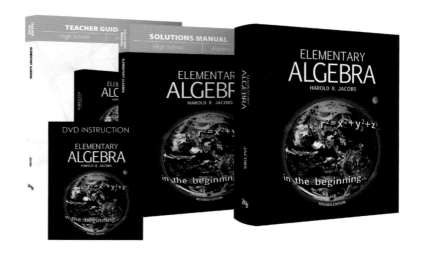

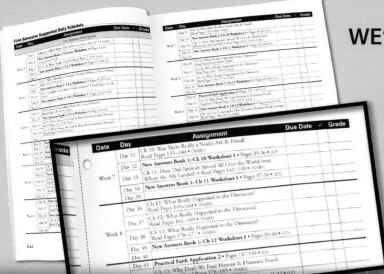

wonders of the HUMAN BODY SERIES

INTRODUCTION TO ANATOMY & PHYSIOLOGY 1

INTRODUCTION TO ANATOMY & PHYSIOLOGY 2

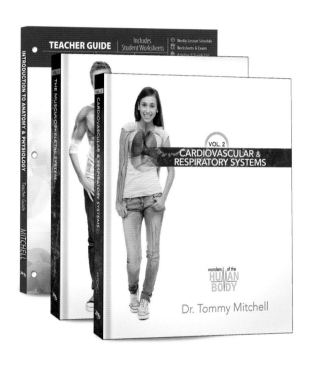

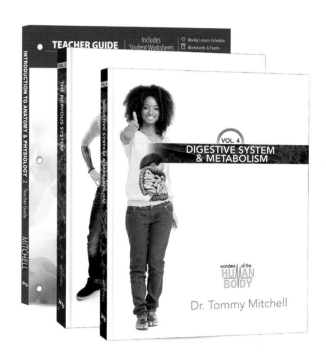

Learn about the musculoskeletal system and the cardio and respiratory systems from the cell level to the systems themselves. There will be no denying that the human body can only be the product of a Master Designer.

3 Book set : 978-0-89051-946-2

Learn about the incredible complexity of the nervous system, where your student will realize that their bodies cannot be the result of chemical accidents occurring over millions of years. They will then study the function of digestion, a highly complex system created by God to transform food into fuel for our energy, something called metabolism, and to take waste from the body. The human body is the greatest creation of an all-knowing Master Designer!

3 Book set : 978-1-68344-145-8